To Live in God

Daily Reflections with
Walter Rauschenbusch

Introduced and edited by
Dennis L. Johnson

JUDSON PRESS
PUBLISHERS SINCE 1824
VALLEY FORGE, PA

Judson Press has made every effort to trace the ownership of all quotes. In the event of a question arising from the use of a quote, we regret any error made and will be pleased to make the necessary correction in future printings and editions of this book.

In the progressive spirit of Walter Rauschenbusch and Helen Barrett Montgomery both, the author and publisher have made minor adaptations to the historic texts to minimize masculine God language (in the case of Rauschenbusch) and to use gender inclusive language for human beings.

Unless otherwise indicated, Bible quotations in this volume are from *The New Testament in Modern English* translated by Helen Barrett Montgomery © 1924 by American Baptist Publication Society. All rights reserved.

The Complete Bible: An American Translation (Goodspeed) translated by J. M. Powis Smith and a group of scholars. The Apocrypha and The New Testament translated by Edgar J. Goodspeed. The University of Chicago Press, Chicago, IL, The Baker & Taylor Company, NY, and The Cambridge University Press, London, © 1939.

The New Revised Standard Version of the Bible (NRSV), copyright © 1989 by the Division of Christian Education of the National Council of the Churches of Christ in the United States of America. Used by permission. All rights reserved.

The Holy Bible, King James Version (KJV).

Cover photo courtesy of the American Baptist Historical Society.
Interior design by Beth Oberholtzer.
Cover design by Danny Ellison.

Library of Congress Cataloging-in-Publication data
Names: Rauschenbusch, Walter, 1861-1918, author. | Johnson, Dennis L., compiler.
Title: To live in God: daily reflections with Walter Rauschenbusch / compiled and
    introduced by Dennis L. Johnson.
Description: Valley Forge, PA: Judson Press, 2020. | Includes bibliographical refer-
    ences. | Summary: "The main thing is to have God; to live in God; to have God live
    in us... that is the blessed life." So declared the founder of the Social Gospel, and
    so forms the hearts of this inspirational collection of Rauschenbusch's thoughts
    and prayers about the spiritual life. Comprised of a scriptural passage, excerpted
    reading, and actual prayer written by Rauschenbusch himself, this volume of 180
    daily reflections will encourage and exhort readers in spiritual growth and social
    action. Organized into three sections of 60 reflections each, the book focuses first
    on the inward journey of solitude, then the outward journey of service, and the
    common journey of solidarity"--Provided by publisher.
Identifiers: LCCN 2019045723 (print) | LCCN 2019045724 (ebook) | ISBN
    9780817018085 (paperback) | ISBN 9780817082079 (ebook)
Subjects: LCSH: Spiritual life--Prayers and devotions. | Christian life--Prayers and
    devotions. | Devotional literature.
Classification: LCC BV4501.3 .R39155 2020 (print) | LCC BV4501.3 ebook) |
    DDC 242/.2--dc23
LC record available at https://lccn.loc.gov/2019045723
LC ebook record available at https://lccn.loc.gov/2019045724

Printed in the U.S.A.
First printing, 2020.

Above all,
this book is lovingly dedicated
to Holly,
who fills my life
with faith, hope, and love,
and the greatest of these is love.

I also give it with gratitude
for the beloved mentors, teachers, soul friends,
colleagues, and congregations
I have walked alongside, learned from, and served with.

Contents

Preface

I was a Baptist minister searching for a Baptist model of spiritual formation and my quest led me to Walter Rauschenbusch. That was thirty years ago during my metropolitan Chicago ministry days as an American Baptist pastor and a Doctor of Ministry student at Northern Baptist Theological Seminary. Over the years my attachment to Rauschenbusch as a spiritual guide deepened and has resulted in the book you are holding in your hands.

The life he lived, the writings he composed, and the prayers he offered have moved me along to live in God more fully, more freely, and more fearlessly. The following readings are offered with the hope that the wisdom of Rauschenbusch will further what it means to live in God and will deepen the spiritual life and vitality of those who take time to ponder and pray his words from a century ago. I know from experience that the words still have power to touch the soul and shape the heart more in the likeness of Christ.

As an effort to root the readings more firmly in the soil of Baptist heritage, I have chosen to include verses from New Testament translations by two Baptist contemporaries of Rauschenbusch. Most of the New Testament verses are from *A Centenary Translation* by Helen Barrett Montgomery (1861–1934), published by Judson Press in 1924. She was the first woman to translate the New Testament from Greek into English and have it professionally published. As a resident of Rochester, NY, she knew and respected Professor Rauschenbusch at Rochester Divinity School and she was a co-worker with another Rochester native, Susan B. Anthony. In 1899 she was the first woman elected to the Rochester School Board, twenty years before women secured the right to vote. In 1921 she was elected the first female president of the Northern Baptist Convention (today ABCUSA), which also made her the first woman president of any American religious denomination. During her term as president, she confronted and resisted an attempted fundamentalist takeover of the Convention with efforts to impose a doctrinal identity and confessional conformity on local Baptist congregations. She brought a message of liberty to her presidency and said that the priority should be on the mission of the church rather than on divisive theological issues. In the Introduction to her translation, she wrote, "The author offers the results of many years of happy work, in deep humility and with a keen sense of the many shortcomings of her work; but in the ardent hope that it may bring to some a fresh sense of the actuality and power of the wonderful records of the One Perfect Life which has ever been lived. In devotion to him who is Savior and Master, she offers this work of love."

Other New Testament verses are from *An American Translation*, the 1923 translation by Baptist minister and New Testament scholar Edgar Goodspeed (1871–1962), who taught and was chairman of the Department of New Testament and Early Christian Literature at the University of Chicago.[1] Edgar Goodspeed's translation was a forerunner to the 1946 Revised Standard Version for which he toiled fifteen years on the translation committee. Of his *American Translation* he said in the Preface, "It has been truly said that any translation of a masterpiece must be a failure, but if this translation can in any measure bring home the great

---

1. The university was established by Baptists, including Goodspeed's father, with action taken on December 3, 1888 by the Executive Board of the American Baptist Education Society. Leading the effort along with Thomas Goodspeed was William Raney Harper and major donor John D. Rockefeller.

living messages of the New Testament a little more widely and forcibly to the life of our time, the translator will be well content."

I have used the New Revised Standard Version for the Hebrew Scripture verses with one exception: The King James Version of Isaiah 61:3 is just too elegant and lovely to turn away from.

A portion of the Introduction has also appeared in my essay, "Walter Rauschenbusch: A Model of Spiritual Formation for Baptist Congregations," published by the American Baptist Historical Society in the Fall 2017 edition of the *American Baptist Quarterly.*

I am deeply grateful to Judson Press for believing that this Rauschenbusch project was worthy of publication. Special and abundant thanks for the gracious guidance, support, and encouragement of Laura Alden, Rebecca Irwin-Diehl, and Lisa Blair, each of whom made the project so much better and the whole experience for me a joyous adventure and delight.

The late Irish spirituality author and poet John O'Donohue said, "A book is a path of words which takes the heart in new directions."[2] My desire with this book as a path of words is that your heart will be taken to a deeper sense of God's presence within you, a growing attentiveness to God's presence and activity in the world beyond you, and a fresher encounter with and experience of Jesus Christ that will spiritually form you in his image, with Walter Rauschenbusch as a guide on a journey to live in God.

Dennis L. Johnson
Pentecost 2019
Lexington, Kentucky

---

2. John O'Donohue, *Beauty: The Invisible Embrace* (New York: HarperCollins Publishers, 2004), 25.

The Blessed Life

The main thing is
to have God;
to live in God;
to have God live in us;
to think God's thoughts;
to love what God loves
and hate what God hates;
to realize God's presence;
to feel God's holiness
and to be holy
because God is holy;
to feel God's goodness
in every blessing of our life
and even in its tribulations;
to be happy and trustful;
to join in the great purposes of God
and to be lifted to greatness of vision
and faith and hope with God—
that is the blessed life.

Walter Rauschenbusch
"The Culture of the Spiritual Life"
1897

Introduction

Returning from travel abroad, Walter Rauschenbusch was met one day at Ellis Island by a friend who came to help him through customs; the deafness he developed during the 1880s made communication difficult for Rauschenbusch. According to his former student, private secretary, and official biographer, Dores Sharpe, the friend explained to the customs officer the challenges Rauschenbusch faced because of his loss of hearing and asked the officer to be sensitive to his condition. The officer asked, "Who did you say he was?" "Professor Walter Rauschenbusch," the friend answered. "Is he the duck that writes them prayers?" "Yes, he's the man." "Well," said the officer, "they're damn good prayers. I'll pass him as quickly as possible."[3]

In his biography, Sharpe also quotes comments about Rauschenbusch made on the tenth anniversary of his New York City ministry in Hell's Kitchen. William Newton Clarke, professor of theology at Hamilton (Colgate) Theological Seminary, wrote, "I think of him with great tenderness. Rarely have I known a man of such strength of mind, such sweetness of spirit, such brightness of humor, such breadth of interest, and such brave earnestness in behalf of whatever is true and holy." On the same occasion, a butcher who spoke on behalf of the German Baptist congregation Rauschenbusch served said, "We have found in him more that is Christlike than in any human being we have ever

---

3. Dores Robinson Sharpe, *Walter Rauschenbusch* (New York: Macmillan Company, 1942), 284.

met."[4] Such was the impact of Walter Rauschenbusch in his time. From customs officer to seminary professor to local butcher, his life and writings touched people, influenced theology, challenged economics, agitated fellow Christians, altered politics, transformed lives, and reformed society. From the poor to the privileged, from the exploited to the powerful, from the down-and-out to the high-and-mighty, from common laborers to corporate leaders, the being and doing, the words and work of Walter Rauschenbusch had an effect on individuals and social systems, on hearts and minds, on the way things were and the way things ought to be.

Now one hundred years after his death, this caring pastor and social prophet, this Baptist forbearer given a commemorative day on the liturgical calendar of the Episcopal Church (July 2), continues to set an example for what it means to follow Jesus and grow in his likeness, which is the essence of spiritual formation. As M. Robert Mulholland, Jr., tells us, spiritual formation is "a process of being conformed to the image of Christ for the sake of others."[5] While Rauschenbusch is appropriately looked to as one who formulated a theology of the social gospel, the dominant subject of his memorable writing, we must not overlook what he believed and instructed and modeled about nurturing the inward journey and life with God. My own early perception of Rauschenbusch was restricted and narrow, identifying him exclusively with the social justice mandate of the gospel, which he boldly proclaimed and faithfully embodied. I discovered, however, that I was missing the seldom-appreciated and little-discussed dimension of his life and thought dealing with cultivating communion with God, conforming to the image of Christ, and enriching

---

4. Ibid., 78, 79.

5. M. Robert Mulholland, Jr., *Invitation to a Journey* (Downers Grove, IL: Intervarsity Press, 1993), 15.

the life of the Spirit, which included the outward journey of compassionate service for justice, peace, and freedom.

He perceived the need for religious leaders to "give to modern men the inestimable boon of experiencing God as a joy and a power, and of living in him as their fathers did."[6] This can come about with a spirituality in the mold of Rauschenbusch, a spirituality which is deeply personal and passionately social, contemplative and active, experiential and communal, inward and outward, faithfully Baptist and wholeheartedly ecumenical; a spirituality that holds together the inner spiritual life of the person and the corporate social life of humanity. "Only a large faith built on generous, gigantic lines will win the thoughtful men and women of the future,"[7] he wrote in telling why he was a Baptist. He has become part of the magnificent body of truth in the Christian tradition and a source of guidance in spiritual formation and faithfulness to the gospel of Christ and the kingdom.

Raised and nurtured in the pietistic tradition, Walter Rauschenbusch was born in 1861 in America and was a second-generation Baptist preceded by five generations of Lutherans in Germany. The pietistic thread of influence shaped him early and, while he expanded beyond it, he never abandoned it.

The revivalism of Charles Finney, with its emphasis on sanctification, and the sermons of D. L. Moody, which called for personal experience of God in conversion, were formative influences on Rauschenbusch. He collected Moody's sermons between 1886 and 1890 and translated to German many of the gospel songs written by Moody and Ira Sankey. He powerfully witnessed to his own conversion experience

---

6. Rauschenbusch, *Christianizing the Social Order* (New York: Macmillan Company, 1912), 118.

7. Rauschenbusch, "Why I Am a Baptist," *The Baptist Leader* (January 1958), 8.

of Christ, an encounter which came at age seventeen. Of that transformative experience, he wrote:

> Now, that religious experience was a very true one, although I have no doubt that there was a great deal in it that was foolish, that I had to get away from, and that was untrue. And yet, such as it was, it was of everlasting value to me. It turned me permanently, and I thank God with all my heart for it. It was a tender, mysterious experience. It influenced my soul down to its depth.[8]

It was out of this deep personal experience that he entered parish ministry, which brought its own spiritually-shaping influence on his formation.

He served summer pastorates in Louisville, Kentucky, at the German-speaking Baptist church while studying at Rochester Theological Seminary in New York. Reflecting upon his first summer pastorate at age 24, he later wrote:

> I wanted to do hard work for God. Indeed, one of the great thoughts that came upon me was that I ought to follow Jesus Christ in my personal life, and die over again his death. I felt that every Christian ought to participate in the dying of the Lord Jesus Christ, and in that way help to redeem humanity, and it was that thought that gave my life its fundamental direction in the doing of Christian work.[9]

His eleven years (1886–1897) as pastor of the Second German Baptist Church in the Hell's Kitchen neighborhood of New York City continued to form and inform his journey inward and movement outward, his personal spirituality and social spirituality. The extreme poverty of the area along with disease, crime, crowded tenements, unemployment, and malnutrition challenged him personally. He

---

8. Paul M. Minus, *Walter Rauschenbusch: American Reformer* (New York: Macmillan Publishing Company, 1988), 17.

9. Sharpe, 57.

came ready to save souls; he soon realized that there was more to be saved than souls. The young pastor recognized that the neighborhood was not "a safe place for saved souls,"[10] which convinced him of the demand for social salvation along with personal salvation. It was an awakening that would continually challenge him as a Christian and an American and which he used to persistently confront all Christians and Americans.

He returned to Rochester Theological Seminary as a professor in 1897 to begin what would become twenty-one years of profound impact in the classroom and with his writing, sharing his scholarship and passion and prophetic voice.

Rauschenbusch's passion for social transformation was the imperative of his deep spirituality and life with God. His social activism arose from his inner life. His compassionate life emerged from his contemplative life. In 1900 he cautioned about the danger and decaying effect on the church which would result from replacing the personal and affective with social engagement, declaring, "With many, I fear, the religious habits and the intercourse with God have waned as the social interest grew . . . The souls filled with the life of God are the fountains from which all life-giving impulses flow out into the life of society."[11] Whenever the social overshadows the personal, he added, ". . . even the faintest reinforcement of the spiritual life is seized with pathetic eagerness; and when some really strong religious soul gives utterance to original experiences, the general heart-hunger is unmistakable."[12] It was this persistent emphasis of social salvation and reform beginning from within the soul's communion with God that compelled him to present in 1910 his *Prayers of the Social Awakening*.

---

10. Ibid., 61.

11. Rauschenbusch, *Selected Writings*, Winthrop S. Hudson, editor (New York: Paulist Press, 1984), 123, 124.

12. Ibid., 124.

Rauschenbusch found the title of the seventeenth-century spiritual classic by Henry Scougal a favorite definition of religion as "the life of God in the soul of man." Rauschenbusch used this expression as the title for a speech on personal religion he gave in 1900 at the New York State Conference on Religion.[13] Of all the presenters, he alone was asked to speak on personal religion. All other presentations were on social salvation. As Rauschenbusch noted in his address, the conference meant to

> include within its circumference the most pressing religious interests of our time. But of the seven sessions this is the only one devoted to those questions that used to be the chief and almost exclusive topics of discussion in religious assemblies. We must not neglect the personal religious life. . . . My thoughts have turned mainly to the strength and value of the religious instinct in man . . . ; on the instinct that seeks God and on the God that satisfies the instinct. . . . We have realized religion. We live; yet no longer we; it is now the life of God in the soul of man.[14]

The direct consciousness of divine presence as transcendent reality mediated through the physical, aesthetic, moral, and social dimensions of human awareness and the awareness of the inner light of Christ is the spiritual experience and the pursuit of a mystic as seen in Rauschenbusch. He had such personal experiences of grace and he encouraged such experiences in others.

When experiential knowledge of God as personal religion is vital, it opens out into passionate social engagement and ethics. Rauschenbusch suggested that ". . . any decline of our spiritual life, if it lasted long enough, brought in its train a corresponding decline in our moral vigor. Our ideals paled; our love for men grew chill; and selfishness and cal-

---

13. Ibid., 122.
14. Ibid., 123, 124, 133.

culation took possession."[15] The inward and outward are linked, which prevents either a private pietism or humanistic activism. This outward movement in loving and joyful response to the experience of God prevents spirituality from being locked in private self-centeredness, which Rauschenbusch vigorously and prophetically challenged. The within moves outward and the outward begins within as authentic spirituality. To pigeonhole him as being most notably about social salvation is to overlook what sustained him. The spirituality offered by Walter Rauschenbusch prompts us today to place primary value on experiential knowledge of God which affirms a mysticism that does not detach us from the world but engages society so our lives in Jesus Christ will carry a true witness to grace as the transforming, as well as unmerited, love of God in our human experience.

The journey is not only inward and outward in the spirituality of Walter Rauschenbusch. We also travel the common journey. It was his interest in and appreciation for the Quakers' attentiveness to the Spirit as the Christ within and their commitment to the corporate, and his reading of Loyola, that resulted in Rauschenbusch being shaped in community and his insistence on the working of God through life together. He experienced and witnessed to his sense of communal life in spiritual formation when he took the initiative early in his Hell's Kitchen pastorate to meet each week for Bible study and reflection with two friends, Leighton Williams, pastor of the Amity Baptist Church, and Nathaniel Schmidt, pastor of the Swedish Baptist Church. They also gathered together each Sunday afternoon to share the Lord's Supper. Winthrop Hudson records, "Through the discipline of weekly study, discussion, mutual criticism, and common worship, they sought to clarify their thinking, deepen their devotion, and chart a course by which they might exert a

---

15. Ibid., 126, 127.

united influence."[16] Over time this small gathering gave birth to a larger community expression of communal spiritualty known as "The Brotherhood of the Kingdom" which met annually for twenty years for mutual support, theological reflection, and testing of ideas to advance social justice and peace. The spiritual life for Rauschenbusch was life together, each needing the other, growing with one another in Christ-likeness inwardly and outwardly.

The common journey was also one of being bound in solidarity with all humanity. Submission to God includes yielding to the priority of the common good and the need of others over the individual. The soul is voluntarily social-ized. The submissive heart is other-oriented and communal rather than self-oriented and privatized. To be shaped in the image of Christ and to live life in the likeness of Christ is to stand for the solidarity of humankind without distinc-tion or exclusion. It embraced what Rauschenbusch called "anthropocentric mysticism" which sees the image of God in others. There is no true inward journey with God or out-ward journey of service without the common journey of love and justice, mercy and peace in solidarity with human-ity. The wholeness and holiness of this inward, outward and common journey was, Rauschenbusch said, "the main thing" and he called it "the blessed life."

He identified five ways by which we are shaped in the image of Christ for the sake of others[17] and experience the blessed life. These aspects of cultivating the life of solitude, service, and solidarity are woven throughout the following daily readings.

First, we form spiritually by consecration to Christ and

---

16. Ibid., 12.
17. Four of his articles provide his most specific writing on cultivat-ing the spiritual life. One appeared in *The Rochester Baptist Monthly*, November 1897, and the others were in *The Baptist Union of Chicago*, February 26, March 5, March 12, 1898.

to the purposes of Christ, which involves aligning and realigning our purposes in life and removing obstacles to becoming Christlike.

Second, we form spiritually by attentiveness to and living in the presence of the loving God, resting in God's encompassing companionship and nurturing an ever-deepening sense of practicing the presence of God.

Third, as offered by Rauschenbusch, we form spiritually by "wisely and constantly drawing on the great storehouses of the past for spiritual sustenance and wisdom."[18] The great storehouses of the past included for Rauschenbusch devotional literature, theology, church history, and biographies, with the supreme storehouse, of course, being the Bible.

Fourth, he said that we cultivate the spiritual life and form into the image of Christ by fellowship with women and men whose faith nurtures and challenges us, strengthens and stretches us. No one forms in isolation. In the fellowship of the saints we offer confession and receive forgiveness; we seek guidance and provide direction; we practice discernment and make decisions; we gather to be strengthened and part to serve.

Fifth, we form spiritually by our compassionate service to others and work in the world, which is holy work in daily service to make the reign of God on earth a reality here and now. He said, "The better we know Jesus the more social do his thoughts and aims become."[19] All work in the world becomes an act of seeking and serving first the kingdom and righteousness of God, and Rauschenbusch said that compassionately living and working for peace and justice not only changes the way things are in the world but also make us more Christlike. One is not Jesus-like and leading

---

18. *Writings*, 105.

19. Rauschenbusch, *Christianity and the Social Crisis* (New York: Association Press, 1912), 46.

the Christian life without holy work and service to others. We find ourselves becoming more conformed to the image of Christ as we see the presence of Christ in those we serve.

Inevitably, service as social spirituality in the Spirit of Christ will involve conflict, for it is "a lifelong fight with organized evil."[20] Rauschenbusch was well aware from personal experience that service and suffering are inseparable signs of the cross on the servant. Service in the world identifies the cross as more than an "expedient in the scheme of redemption."[21] He called the cross a law of life. It is a way of life for followers of Jesus. It calls us to a new way of being human in the world as living incarnations of Jesus.

Consecration to Christ and Christ's purposes, practicing the presence of God, drawing on the great storehouses of the past, being in fellowship with others, and working and serving in the world—these five elements as set forth by Rauschenbusch serve as significant pathways for the inward journey, the outward journey, and the common journey.

The Quaker writer Douglas Steere once said that a saint's life at heart is a "life of attention to and abandonment to the besieging love of God."[22] The only claim saints make is the desire to know and serve God, to willingly, trustingly put themselves fully into God's hands. Steere added that the question the saint always asks is not, "*Who* am I?" but "*Whose* am I?" The answer comes back again and again, "I am thine, O Lord," and, as the old hymn adds, "I have heard thy voice, and it told thy love to me." "Whose am I?" was the question Walter Rauschenbusch asked throughout his life and "I am thine, O Lord" was the answer he gave back.

---

20. *Christianizing*, 112.
21. Ibid.
22. Douglas Steere, quoted in E. Glenn Hinson, "What the World Needs Most," *From Our Christian Heritage*, C. Douglas Weaver, ed. (Macon, GA: Smyth & Helwys Publishing, Inc., 1997), 305.

At a time when wealth was concentrated in the hands of a few, to an industrialized, militarized, polarized society, which sounds so familiar to our time and society, Walter Rauschenbusch was a prophetic voice of protest and a fearless follower of Christ whose lectures in the classroom and sermons from the pulpit, whose books and articles, whose prayers and presence, whose being and doing turned heads and touched hearts and served to bring forth God's reign of justice and mercy and love. Today his influence endures. His model of discipleship and spirituality is meaningful, in the words of Fosdick, "for the living of these days." While he died a century ago, the mark he left and the impact he made are very much alive.

That Hell's Kitchen butcher, brother Julius Dietz, who spoke with humble eloquence of his pastor's Christlikeness, went on to say,

> "We have in him a perfectly fearless preacher, one who cares nothing about criticism of any sort, but who always stands up and in a manly, fearless way, teaches and adheres strictly to Christ's teaching, and you will probably all agree with me when I say that because of being this style of teacher, thoughts and ideas pertaining to the Christian life have been instilled into our minds and hearts and have taken root there, that have been entirely foreign to us previous to his coming here. Regarding his labors outside the church I might also touch upon them had I the time. His work among the poor, his work as a writer, his labor in connection with our new church, and in many other directions, and when I review all of it, and feel he is our pastor, my heart says, 'Praise God from whom all blessing flow' who has placed our brother among us."[23]

The pages that follow form an invitation to spend six months in daily readings with Walter Rauschenbusch, our

---

23. Quoted in Donovan E. Smucker, "The Rauschenbusch Story," *Foundations* 2: (January 1959), 6, 7.

brother whom God placed among us, and to reflect with him on the Christian's inward journey, outward journey, and common journey. A Scripture passage is provided each day to begin the time of reflection by dwelling in the Word to prepare for pondering the words of Rauschenbusch. Formative questions to ask in the dwelling and ponderings are, "What speaks to me? What troubles me? What am I being told about God, about myself, about others? What am I being called to become or to do?" Each daily reading ends with portions of those "damn good prayers" he published as *Prayers of the Social Awakening*. The daily pattern is simply prepare, ponder, and pray, with the hope that true worship, which he said is to live continually "in the consciousness of the love and nearness of God, to merge all our desires and purposes in his will, to walk humbly before him and justly and lovingly"[24] with all people, will shape our inward communion with God and outward obedience to God in the likeness of Jesus Christ for the sake of others with whom we share the road. This is the blessed life.

---

24. "Why I Am a Baptist," 14.

The Inward Journey

*To Live in God
and Have God Live in Us*

This world of ours has length and breadth,
A superficial and horizontal world.
When I am with God
I look deep down and high up.
And all is changed.
The world of mortals is made of jangling noises.
With God it is a great silence.
But that silence is a melody
Sweet as the contentment of love,
Thrilling as a touch of flame.

Walter Rauschenbusch
"The Little Gate to God"
1918

*The message of God is a living and active force, sharper than
any double-edged sword, piercing through soul and spirit,
and joints and marrow, and keen in judging the thoughts
and purposes of the mind.* (Hebrews 4:12, Goodspeed)

Holiness of Life

MARK 6:30-32

Come apart to a quiet spot, a solitary place.

We must grow in holiness of life. Holiness is more than goodness. Holiness is goodness on fire. It is goodness created by fellowship with God. Am I wrong in my impression, or is it true, that in our busy, bustling Christian life, the quiet, gentle elements of spiritual communion, the devoutness of a secret walk with God, are imperiled and to some extent lost? We do much for God, but we do not rest much in God. I have known some rare souls who breathed forth that devoutness in all their lives, and what a power they exert! They are like a personification of the still, small voice which Elijah heard.

Our Master, the sense of our shortcomings is quick within us and we seek thy pardon.

The Power of Silence

PSALM 62

For God alone my soul waits in silence. (NRSV)

I would plead for more spiritual retirement, for more moments when the door of our closet is shut behind us, and the door of our heart too is closed to the world and its exacting cares, and we enter into the secret of God's presence. We believe in the sanctifying power of confession and testimony. Is there not a sanctifying power in silence, too?

We praise thee for the hours of holy quiet in which we crossed the threshold of thy presence and listened to the inner voice in the most holy place.

Living as a Child of God

JOHN 1:8-13

*But to all who receive him, to them he has
given the right to become children of God,
even to those who trust in his name.*

Realize often the presence of God. It is the first article
of religious belief that there is a living God. It is the first
act of religious life to realize God and come into contact
with God. It is a mighty act of faith every time . . . If your
thoughts are often of the living God, if God's fatherly care
is your trust, if God's will is your final law, if God's communion is your joy, you are living as a child of God, as a
possessor of the spiritual and eternal life. Therefore practice
the presence of God.

*O Thou great companion of our souls, comfort us by the
sense of thy presence in the hours of spiritual isolation.
Give us a single eye for duty. Guide us by the voice within.*

Turn to God

PSALM 4

*When you are disturbed, do not sin; ponder it and
be silent and put your trust in the LORD.* (NRSV)

Bring God to mind in prayer. Just turn from the world a
moment and think of God. Do so especially when you are
anxious and worn with care. Turn to God and leave your
troubles with God. Many of them will shrink and look
foolishly small when God's light falls on them . . . Turn to
God in your moments of joy and gratitude too. Share them
with God. Apply the social instinct to the best companion
of all, to your God.

*O thou Great Creator of us all, we rejoice that at last we
know thee. All our soul within us is glad because we need
no longer cringe before thee as slaves of holy fear, seeking
to appease thine anger by sacrifice and self-inflicted pain,
but may come like little children, trustful and happy, to
the God of love.*

A Downward Sag

PSALM 51

Have mercy on me, O God, according to your
steadfast love; Create in me a clean heart, O God,
and put a new and right spirit within me. (NRSV)

We must constantly correct our purposes in life. Even if we have surrendered ourselves to the obedience of God, there will be a sagging downward. We begin by seeking first the kingdom of God, and end by taking the glory for ourselves. Our selfishness and pride steals insidiously into everything we do. We can do the most pious things, the most unselfish actions, and appropriate them all to ourselves and take all the holiness out of them. There are distinctions there too fine for the judgment of others, too fine too for our unaided eye. But when we bring them before God in prayer, we can see how things are. Therefore we need to place our aims and motives before God for his scrutiny, praying [for] God to cleanse us from our secret sins. Now and then, too, we ought to consider our life as a whole to see if it is not unconsciously deflecting from the straight line of God's will.

Our Father, we look back on the years that are gone and shame and sorrow come upon us, for the harm we have done to others rises up in our memory to accuse us. Some we have seared with the fire of our lust, and some we have scorched with the heat of our anger. In some we helped to quench the glow of young ideals by our selfish pride and craft, and in some we have nipped the opening bloom of faith by the frost of our unbelief.

Remove the Obstacles

EPHESIANS 4:25–5:2

*Learn then to imitate God as his beloved children,
and to lead lives of love, just as Christ also loved you
and gave himself up for you.*

"Quench not the Spirit"; it is quenched by refusing obedience to its promptings. "Grieve not the Spirit"; it is grieved when we hold fast to things which it hates. Plants must be nurtured by securing for them sunshine and rain, but also by ridding them of the weeds and thistles that absorb the nourishment of the soil. The spiritual life too is fostered by removing the obstacles to it.

May we not hide our sins from thee but overcome them by the stern comfort of thy presence. By this knowledge uphold us in our sorrows and make us patient even amid the unsolved mysteries of the years. Reveal to us the larger goodness and love that speak through the unbending laws of thy world. Through this faith make us the willing equals of all thy other children.

The Law of Love

MARK 12:28-34

Other command greater than these there is none.

To Jesus the law of love was so great and all-inclusive that he felt it summed up and superseded the whole majestic framework of the Jewish law. Jesus transformed the inherited conceptions of God himself by baptizing the Hebrew Jehovah in love and reintroducing the imperious King of Sinai to humanity as the Father whom they might love because he loved them to the death.

Suffer us not to darken thy world by lovelessness, but give us the power of the children of God to bring in the reign of love among all people.

Sharing the Spirit of Jesus

JOHN 13:3-17

*So after he had washed their feet, and had put on
his upper garments again, and taken his place,
he said to them: "Do you understand what I have been
doing to you? I have given you an example, that you
also should do what I have done to you."*

We are Christians in the degree in which we share the spirit
and consciousness of Jesus Christ, conceiving God as Jesus
knew God and seeing human life as Jesus realized it. None
of us has ever done this fully, but on the other hand there
is no one within the domain of Christendom who has not
been influenced by Christ in some way.

*We pray thee, O Lord, for the graces of a pure and holy
life that we may no longer add to the dark weight of the
world's sin that is laid upon thee, but may share with thee
in thy redemptive work.*

Real Worship

PSALM 116

What shall I return to the LORD for all his bounty to me?
I will lift up the cup of salvation and call on the name of
the LORD in the presence of all his people. O LORD,
I am your servant. You have loosed my bonds. (NRSV)

The real worship, the only thing that God really cares for, is a Christlike life. To live all the time in the consciousness of the love and nearness of God, to merge all our desires and purposes in God's will, to walk humbly before God and justly and lovingly with all people, this is the real Christian worship. Without that no prayer, no song, no "divine service" on Sunday is more than discordant noise in the ears of God . . . A loving and pure life is the true liturgy of Christian worship.

Though increase of knowledge bring increase of sorrow, may we turn without flinching to the light and offer ourselves as instruments of thy spirit in bringing order and beauty out of disorder and darkness.

More Than a Baptist

1 CORINTHIANS 3:18-23

*For all things are yours; Paul, Apollos, Cephas, the world,
life, death, things present or things to come; all things
are yours; and you are Christ's, and Christ is God's.*

Baptists are not a perfect denomination. We are capable
of being just as narrow and small as anybody . . . I do not
want to foster Baptist self-conceit, because thereby I should
grieve the Spirit of Christ. I do not want to make Baptists
shut themselves up in their little clamshells and be indifferent to the ocean outside of them. I am a Baptist, but I am
more than a Baptist. All things are mine; whether Francis
of Assisi, or Luther, or Knox, or Wesley; all things are mine
because I am Christ's.

*O God, we pray for thy church. We remember with love
the nurture she gave to our spiritual life in its infancy, the
tasks she set for our growing strength, the influence of the
devoted hearts she gathers, the steadfast power for good
she has exerted.*

The Great Treasure House

1 JOHN 1:1-4

*And the Life was made visible, and we have seen it
and are bearing witness, and are bringing you word
of that Eternal Life which was face to face with the Father
and was made visible to us. And we are writing all this
to you that our joy may be complete.*

God has spoken, not a few times, but as often as God could find a soul capable of hearing his voice; those who heard God told what they heard and thereby encouraged others to listen to the divine voice and give heed to it . . . and some part of this knowledge was under God's providence put into writing and collected in our Bible, which we hold in reverence as a precious gift of God, as the great treasure house of revelations and religious experiences.

Make us worthy to bear thy message. May every word and act be the simple pulsing of a Christian heart.

The Culminating Revelation of God

HEBREWS 1:1-4

He is the reflection of God's glory, and the representation
of his being, and bears up the universe by his mighty word.
(Goodspeed)

It is a glorious truth that God has spoken to mortals; and every fragmentary utterance of prophetic souls, however much it may be colored by their personality and their times, should be precious in our sight if it bears the royal stamp of the divine touch and mission. But we glory in the culminating revelation of God in his Son; in the simplicity and strength of his words; in the obedience and unbroken fellowship of his life, which made him the unsullied mirror of the effulgence of God's glory, the unblurred image of God's substance. He draws us; he masters us; he transforms us. In him we see God; in him we possess God; in him God possesses us.

Fix on the sensitive film of our spirits the image and splendor of Christ which has shone upon us.

Dying Piecemeal

JOHN 12:20-28

*In solemn truth I tell you that except a kernel of wheat
fall into the ground and die, it remains a single kernel;
but if it die it bears a great crop.*

Unselfishness and self-sacrifice seem to me the idea of Christ's life and therefore the expression of God's character. In proportion as they become the dominant facts of our own life, we are conformed to his image. I tell you I am just beginning to believe in the Gospel of the Lord Jesus Christ, not exactly in the shape in which the average person proclaims it as the infallible truth of the Most High, but in a shape that suits my needs, that I have gradually constructed for myself in studying the person and teaching of Christ, and which is still in rapid process of construction. I don't believe that believing any doctrine will do a person any good except so far as it is translated into life. I don't believe that when a person believes in the vicarious death of Christ that death will be imputed to him or her; how can it? But if that person begins to live a Christlike life, that person will find that though there is no cross to be nailed to, he or she will die piecemeal by self-sacrifice just as Christ did even before his crucifixion and then the person is at one with Christ and placed by God in the same category.

*As thou art ever pouring out thy life in sacrificial love,
may we accept the eternal law of the cross and give ourselves to thee and to all people.*

Upheld by the Comforts of God

ISAIAH 43:1-7

When you pass through the waters, I will be with you;
and through the rivers, they shall not overwhelm you;
when you walk through the fire you shall not
be burned, and the flame shall not consume you.
Do not fear, for I am with you. (NRSV)

My life has been physically very lonely and often beset by the consciousness of conservative antagonism. I have been upheld by the comforts of God. Jesus has been to me an inexhaustible source of fresh impulse, life, and courage.

My life would seem an empty shell if my personal religion were left out of it. It has been my deepest satisfaction to get evidence now and then that I have been able to help others to a new spiritual birth. I have always regarded my public work as a form of evangelism, which called for a deeper repentance and a new experience of God's salvation.

If our spirit droops in loneliness, uphold us by thy companionship. When all the voices of love grow faint and drift away, thy everlasting arms will still be there.

Silence

PSALM 131

I have calmed and quieted my soul. (NRSV)

Is there not an element which we can adopt in the quiet Quaker meetings, in which there is no demand for speaking and no sense of failure if all are silent, but which are occasionally stirred like the pool of Bethesda by a rippling touch of an angel's wing? Can we not learn something from the retreats which the Catholic Church provides for her priests, in which the souls are led merely to meditation and adoration?

We thank thee for our senses by which we can see the splendor of the morning, and hear the jubilant songs of love, and smell the breath of the springtime.

Enter into God

PSALM 23:1-3

*He makes me lie down in green pastures; He leads me
beside still waters; he restores my soul.* (NRSV)

In the castle of my soul is a little garden gate,
Whereat, when I enter, I am in the presence of God.
In a moment, in the turning of a thought,
    I am where God is,
This is a fact . . .
When I enter into God, all life has a meaning.
Without asking I know; my desires are even now fulfilled,
My fever is gone in the great quiet of God.
My troubles are but pebbles on the road,
My joys are like the everlasting hills.
So it is when I step through the gate of prayer from time
    into eternity.

*O God, we praise thy holy name. Be with us through all
the strain of the days that are before us. Brood over us
with thy Holy Spirit. Shine upon us, thou sun of our life,
even in the valley of the shadow, and may the sun of faith
never die in our hearts.*

The Homeland of My Soul

PSALM 23:4-6

Even though I walk through the darkest valley,
I fear no evil; for you are with me. Goodness and mercy
shall follow me all the days of my life. (NRSV)

When I am in the consciousness of God,
My fellowmen are not far-off and forgotten,
   but close and strangely dear.
Those whom I love have a mystic value.
They shine, as if a light were glowing within them.
Even those who frown on me and love me not
Seem part of the great scheme of good.
(Or else they seem like stray bumble-bees
   buzzing at a window,
Headed the wrong way, yet seeking the light.)
So it is when my soul steps through the garden gate
   into the presence of God.
Big things become small, and small things become great.
The near becomes far, and the future is near.
The lowly and despised is shot through with glory . . .
God is the substance of all revolutions;
When I am in God, I am in the Kingdom of God
And the homeland of my Soul.

Do thou reward thy servants with a glad sense of their
own eternal worth and in the heat of the day do thou
show them the spring by the wayside that flows from the
eternal silence of God and gives new light to the eyes of
all who drink of it.

Thirsting for God

PSALM 42

Why are you cast down, O my soul, and why are you disquieted within me? Hope in God; for I shall again praise him, my help and my God. (NRSV)

We have probably all felt the poignant sense of want and loss when our religious life declined and we remembered our first love from which we had fallen; or when the gray mist of doubt crept between us and the face of our God, and we feared that our faith might be lost to us forever. At such times the words of the Psalmist did not seem over-drawn: "As the heart panteth after the water brooks, so panteth my soul after thee, O God! My soul thirsts for God, for the living God."

Comfort and ease those who toss wakeful on a bed of pain, or whose aching nerves crave sleep and find it not. Save them from evil or despondent thoughts in the long darkness, and teach them so to lean on thy all-pervading life and love, that their souls may grow tranquil and their bodies, too, may rest.

The Living Experience of God

HOSEA 6:1-3

Come, let us return to the LORD; let us know,
let us press on to know the LORD; his appearing
is as sure as the dawn. (NRSV)

Personal religion has a supreme value for its own sake, not merely as a feeder of social morality, but as the highest unfolding of life itself, as the blossoming of our spiritual nature. Spiritual regeneration is the most important fact in any life history. A living experience of God is the crowning knowledge attainable to a human mind.

Multiply the God-conquered souls who open their hearts gladly to the light that makes us free, for all creation shall be in travail till these sons and daughters of God attain their glory.

The Ultimate Meaning of Life

JOHN 17:1-5

*Eternal life means knowing you as the only true God,
and knowing Jesus your messenger as Christ.* (Goodspeed)

Each one of us needs the redemptive power of religion for our own sake, for on the tiny stage of the human soul all the vast world tragedy of good and evil is reenacted. In the best social order that is conceivable we will still smolder with lust and ambition, and be lashed by hate and jealousy as with the whip of a slave driver. No material comfort and plenty can satisfy the restless soul in us and give us peace with ourselves. All who have made test of it agree that religion alone holds the key to the ultimate meaning of life, and each of us must find our way into the inner mysteries alone . . . Religion is eternal life in the midst of time and transcending time.

Suffer us not by thoughtless condemnation or selfish opposition to weaken the arm and chill the spirit of those who strive for the redemption of humankind.

The Trembling Compass-Needle Pointing to Eternity

EPHESIANS 1:15-23

I am praying that the eyes of your heart may be flooded with light so that you may understand what is the hope of God's calling.

When we reel under the first shock of new doubts; when our own spiritual life is low and the inward oracle in our soul is almost dumb, we do well to realize how much we owe to social religion. The accumulated deposit of the spiritual life of the past, the inspired utterances of stronger souls, the institutional edifice and the history of the church, and the living contact with devoted souls reassure us and carry us safely through the vulnerable period of our spiritual metamorphosis.

And so we contemplate with profound awe this trembling compass-needle pointing out into eternity, the religious life in our souls. It contradicts our worldly common sense, crowds back our most imperious passions, thwarts our ambitions, humbles us in the dust, sets us unending tasks and rewards us with a crown of thorns. And yet we love it, reverence it, desire it; and no dearer gift could come to us than absolute certitude that all it tells us is truth.

Thou alone art our Redeemer, for thy lifting arms were about us and thy persistent voice was in our hearts as we slowly climbed up from savage darkness and cruelty.

The Life of God in Our Souls

ISAIAH 40:21-31

*Have you not known? Have you not heard? The LORD
is the everlasting God, the Creator of the ends of the earth.
He does not faint or grow weary. He gives power to the faint,
and strengthens the powerless. Those who wait for the
LORD shall renew their strength.* (NRSV)

The life of God in our souls lends grandeur to the scattered and fragmentary purposes of our life by gathering them into a single all-comprehending aim—the kingdom of God, which is the hallowing of God's name and the doing of God's will. It guarantees that our aspirations are not idle dreams nor our sacrifices fruitless toil, but that they are of God and through God and unto God, and shall have their fulfillment and reward. When the vast world numbs us with a sense of helplessness and ignorance, prayer restores our sense of worth by the consciousness of kinship with the Lord of all. Even when our strength is broken, when our hopes are frustrated and nature seems to cast us aside, we can trust and wait. By holding up the will of the Holy One as the norm of action and character, religion spurs us on to endless growth.

*O Lord, thou knowest that we are sore stricken and heavy
of heart. We beseech thee to uphold us by thy comfort.
Thou wert the God of our fathers and mothers, and in all
these years thine arm has never failed us, for our strength
has ever been as our days.*

The Light of God Within

LUKE 15:11-25

While he was yet a great way off, his father saw him and was moved with compassion, and ran and fell on his neck and kissed him. "This son of mine was dead and is alive again— he was lost and is found." So they began to make merry.

The wind that blows, the birds that sing, and the crimson flood of life and nourishment that throbs in our pulses are all part of the great cosmic life. The force of God is in the movements of matter and the thrills of organic life. But they all act as they must.

In the ocean of the universe floats the little bark of human personality, part of it all, and yet an entity in itself. It knows; it wills; it is conscious of itself over against the world, and even over against God. More and more clearly the thoughts of God are mirrored by the reflecting human intellect, illuminated by God's own mind, the light of God in the human soul.

But to the human personality comes a faint and far call, sweeter than the rhythm of the spheres, the voice of the Father of spirits calling to a child. Our souls give answer by eternal longing and homesickness. The husks of necessity drop from our hands, and we long for the bread of freedom and peace in the eternal habitation of our Father. And with that conscious turning to God, we leave slavery and enter kinship as daughters and sons of God. We have realized religion. We live; yet no longer we; it is now the life of God in the soul of mortals.

We praise thee, O Lord, for that mysterious spark of thy light within us, the human intellect, for thou hast kindled it in the beginning and by the breath of thy Spirit it has grown to flaming power in humanity.

Like an Emancipation

COLOSSIANS 1:13-14

God has delivered us out of the dominion of the darkness,
and transplanted us into the kingdom of his dear Son.

Evangelism is the attack of redemptive energy in the sphere of personal life. It comes to us shamed by the sense of guilt and baffled by moral failure and rouses us to a consciousness of our high worth and eternal destiny. It transmits the faith of the Christian Church in a loving and gracious God who is willing to forgive and powerful to save. It teaches us to pray, curing our soul by affirming over and over a triumphant faith, and throwing it open to mysterious spiritual powers, which bring joy, peace, and strength beyond ourselves. It sets before us a code of moral duty to quicken and guide our conscience. It puts us inside of a group of like-minded people who exercise social restraint and urge us on.

When all this is wisely combined, it constitutes a spiritual reinforcement of incomparable energy. It acts like an emancipation. It gives us a sense of freedom and newness.

O God, we beseech thee to save us from the distractions of vanity and the false lure of inordinate desires. If the fierce tide of greed beats against the breakwaters of our soul, may we rest at peace in thy higher contentment.

Seeing the Invisible

HEBREWS 11:1-3; 12:1-3

Faith means the assurance of what we hope for; it is our conviction about things that we cannot see. (Goodspeed)

The writer of Hebrews saw the history of humanity summed up in the live spirits who had the power of projection into the future. Faith is the quality of mind which sees things before they are visible, which acts on ideals before they are realities, and which feels the distant city of God to be more dear, substantial, and attractive than the edible and profitable present. So the writer calls on Christians to take up the same manner of life, and compares them with those running a race in an amphitheater packed with all the generations of the past who are watching them make their record, and bids them keep their eyes on Jesus who starts them at the line and will meet them at the goal, and who has set the pace for good and fleet people for all time. Have we left Jesus behind us by this time?

Send us forth with the pathfinders of humanity to lead thy people another day's march toward the land of promise.

From Old Habits to New Life

JOHN 3:1-21

*I tell you, no one can see the Kingdom of God unless he
is born over again from above!* (Goodspeed)

We call our religious crisis "conversion" when we think of
our own active break with old habits and associations and
our turning to a new life. We call the change "regeneration"
when we think of it as an act of God within us, creating a
new life.

The classic passage on regeneration connects it with the
kingdom of God. Only an inward new birth will enable us
to "see the Kingdom of God" and to "enter the Kingdom of
God." The larger vision and the larger contact both require
a new development of our spirit. In our unregenerate condition the consciousness of God is weak, occasional, and
suppressed. The more Jesus Christ becomes dominant in us,
the more does the light and life of God shine steadily in us,
and create a religious personality which we did not have.
Life is lived under a new synthesis.

*Grant that in us the faith in thy love may shine through
our life with such persuasive beauty that some who still
creep in the dusk of fear may stand erect as free sons and
daughters of God, and that others who now through
unbelief are living as orphans in an empty world may
stretch out their hands to thee and find thee.*

The Lord's Supper and Our Supreme Allegiance

LUKE 22:1-6, 14-23

The high priests and the Scribes continually sought means to put Jesus to death. And when the hour was come Jesus sat down, and the twelve apostles with him, and he said to them: "With desire have I longed to eat this Passover with you before I suffer."

In the Lord's Supper we re-affirm our supreme allegiance to our Lord who taught us to know God as our common parent and to realize that all men and women are our brothers and sisters. In the midst of a world full of divisive selfishness we thereby accept kinship as the ruling principle of our life and undertake to put it into practice in our private and public activities. We abjure the selfish use of power and wealth for the exploitation of our fellows. We dedicate our lives to establishing the kingdom of God and to winning humankind to its laws. In contemplation of the death of our Lord we accept the possibility of risk and loss as our share of service. We link ourselves to his death and accept the obligation of the cross.

Grant us growth of spiritual vision, that with the passing years we may enter into the fullness of this our faith.

God Is in the Growth

COLOSSIANS 1:3-6, 9-12

*I have never ceased to pray for you, asking God to fill you
with the knowledge of his will with every kind of wisdom
and spiritual insight; that you may walk worthy of the Lord;
that you may be fruitful in every kind of good work,
and may increase in the knowledge of God.*

It is the untaught and pagan mind which sees God's presence only in miraculous and thundering action; the more Christian our intellect becomes, the more we see God in growth. By insisting on organic development, we shall follow the lead of Jesus when, in his parables of the sower and of the seed growing secretly, he tried to educate his disciples away from catastrophes to an understanding of organic growth. We shall also be following the lead of the fourth gospel, which translated the terms of eschatology into the operation of present spiritual forces. We shall be following the lead of the Church in bringing the future hope down from the clouds and identifying it with the Church; except that we do not confine it to the single institution of the Church, but see the coming of the kingdom of God in all ethical and spiritual progress of humankind.

Grant that even the sins of my past may yield me added wisdom and tenderness to help those who are tempted.

Being Saved

PHILIPPIANS 2:1-11

Let this mind be in you which was also in Christ Jesus,
who emptied himself of his glory when he was born in
human likeness; he humbled himself in his obedience even
to death; yes, and to death on a cross.

The cross is the monumental fact telling of grace and inviting repentance and humility.

The death of Christ was the conclusive and effective expression of the love of Jesus Christ for God and humanity, and his complete devotion to the kingdom of God. The more his personality was understood to be the full and complete expression of the character of God, the more did his death become the assurance and guarantee that God loves us, forgives us, and is willing to do all things to save us.

We can either be saved by non-ethical sacramental methods or by absorbing the moral character of Jesus into our own character. Let everyone judge which is the salvation he or she wants.

O Lord, we lift our hearts to thee and pray that they be
kept clean of evil passion by the power of forgiving love.
If any slight or wrong still rankles in our souls, help us to
pluck it out and to be healed of thee.

God Has Borne Our Sins

HOSEA 11:1-9

How can I give you up? How can I hand you over?
My heart recoils within me; my compassion grows
warm and tender. I am God and no mortal, the Holy One
in your midst, and I will not come in wrath. (NRSV)

Through his sufferings, Jesus came into full understanding of God's attitude toward malignant sin and adopted it. God's attitude is combined of opposition and love. God has always borne the brunt of human sin while loving us. God too has been gagged and cast out by humans. God has borne our sins with a resistance which never yields and yet is always patient. Within human limits Jesus acted as God acts. The non-resistance of Jesus, so far from being a strange or erratic part of his teaching, is an essential part of his conception of life and of his God-consciousness. When we explain it away or belittle it, we prove that our spirit and his do not coalesce.

Grant that by the insight of love we may understand our brothers and sisters in their wrong, and if their souls are sick, to bear with them in pity and to save them in the gentle spirit of our Master.

That Kind of God

LUKE 15:1-10

Now all the tax collectors and sinners continued to draw near to him, and to listen to him. And the Pharisees and Scribes began to complain, saying, "He is welcoming sinners and eating with them!"

The human value of Jesus' love was translated into higher terms by the belief that Christ revealed and expressed the heart and mind of God. If Christ stood for saving pity and tender mercy and love that seeks the lost, then God must be that kind of a God. Jesus' death effectively made God a God of love to the simplest soul, and that has transformed the meaning of the universe and the whole outlook of humankind. Love has been written into the character of God and into the ethical duty of humanity; not only common love, but self-sacrificing love. And it was the death of Christ which furnished the chief guarantee for the love of God and the chief incentive to self-sacrificing love in human beings.

Eternally loving God, we thank thee for the human love which is the food of our hearts.

We Live on Grace

ROMANS 5:1-5

*Since we stand justified as a result of faith, let us
continue to enjoy the peace we have with God through
our Lord Jesus Christ. Through him also we have had our
access into this grace in which we have taken our stand,
and are exulting in hope of the glory of God.*

Since we live in the fellowship of a God of love, we are
living in a realm of grace as friends and children of God.
We do not have to earn all we get by producing merit. We
live on grace and what we do is slight compared with what
is done for us. The great religious characters are those who
escaped from themselves and learned to depend on God.
Self-earned righteousness and pride in self are the marks
of religious individualism. Humility is the capacity to realize that we count for little in ourselves and must take our
place in the larger fellowship of life. Therefore humility and
dependence on grace are social virtues.

*Our Father, we remember those who must wake that we
may sleep. We thank thee for their faithfulness and sense
of duty. Grant that we may realize how dependent the
safety of our loved ones and the comforts of our life are
on these our brothers and sisters, that so we may think
of them with love and gratitude and help to make their
burden lighter.*

The Source of Our Life

PHILIPPIANS 4:10-13

*I have learned how to be contented with
the condition I am in. I have learned the secret,
in any and all conditions.* (Goodspeed)

Spiritual growth comes by prayer and meditation; by dwelling in the ripening sunshine of God; by opening your soul to the Infinite and Eternal; by what Jeremy Taylor calls, "the practice of the presence of God"*; by fixing your eyes on the earthly figure of our Lord Jesus Christ and drawing strength from his risen presence. So for us there is a renewing and life-giving touch in contact with Christ, the Source of our life. "I can do all things through him that strengthens me."

Grant us the grace of a quiet and humble mind, and may we learn of Jesus to be meek and lowly of heart. In the press of life may we pass from duty to duty in tranquility of heart and spread thy quietness to all who come near.

---

* Jeremy Taylor (1613–1667,) Anglican Bishop of Down and Common in Ireland. *Holy Living*, 1650.

Strike Roots Deep in the Past

HEBREWS 11:29-40

It was for us that God had in store some better thing,
so that apart from us they should not be perfected.

Growth lies in wisely and constantly drawing on the great storehouses of the past for spiritual sustenance and wisdom. We have a great storehouse of thought and inspiration in the Bible, in the history of the Christian Church, in the biographies of her heroes, in the choice fruitage of her devotional literature. Let us strike our roots deep into the past and we grow sturdy, wise, and fit to work.

As the happy memories of the years when we were young together rise up to cheer us, may we feel anew how closely our lives were wrought into one another in their early making, and what a treasure we have had. Whatever new friendships we may form, grant that the old loves may abide to the end and grow ever sweeter with the ripening years.

So Salvation Came to Me

2 TIMOTHY 1:1-12

*Join with me in suffering for the gospel by the power of God.
He has saved us and called us with a holy calling, not
dealing with us according to our works, but according
to his purpose and grace which he gave us in Christ Jesus
before the beginning of time.*

I learned to pray as a little boy at my mother's knee. When I was leaving boyhood behind me, and the seriousness of life began to come over me, I felt the call of God, and after a long struggle extending through several years, I submitted my will to God's law. Henceforth God was consciously present in my life, and this gave it a sense of solemnity and worth. This gave a decisive reinforcement to my will, and turned my life in the direction of service and, when necessary self-sacrifice; so salvation came to me.

O God, we offer thee praise and benediction for the sweet ministries of motherhood in human life. We bless thee for our mothers who built up our lives by theirs. We thank thee for their tireless love, for their voiceless prayers, for the agony with which they followed us through our sins and won us back, for the Christly power of sacrifice and redemption in mother-love.

A Second Great Struggle

1 CORINTHIANS 2:6-16

The Spirit fathoms everything, even the depths of God.
No one understands the thoughts of God but the Spirit of God.
These disclosures we impart in words the Spirit teaches, giving
spiritual truth a spiritual form. (Goodspeed)

When I came to intellectual maturity I had a second great struggle for salvation. During my theological education I was confronted with the choice between the imposing authority of human traditions and the self-evidencing power of God's living word. The former offered a restful dependence on outward authority; the latter brought a never-ending quest for a holy light that always moved forward. This was the personal religious problem of faith applied to intellectual duty. I now had to lean back on the living Spirit of God for support in my intellectual work, and felt God's cooperation. This extended the area of personal religion in my life. I am inexpressibly grateful that I made the choice aright.

We remember with gratitude to thee the godly teachers of our own youth who won our hearts to higher purposes by the sacred contagion of their life. May the strength and beauty of Christlike service be plainly wrought in the lives of their successors, that our children may not want for strong models of devout personhood on whom their characters can be molded.

From Sin to Salvation

COLOSSIANS 3:8-17

Strip off the old self with its doings, and put on that new self which is continually made over according to the likeness of its Creator. In it, Christ is all, and in us all.

If sin is selfishness, salvation must be a change which turns us from self to God and humanity. Our sinfulness consisted in a selfish attitude, in which we were at the center of the universe, and God and all our human kindred were means to serve our pleasures, increase our wealth, and set off our egotisms. Complete salvation, therefore, would consist in an attitude of love in which we would freely co-ordinate our life with the life of others in obedience to the loving impulses of the spirit of God; thus taking our part in a divine organism of mutual service.

Grant us the grace to leave the earth fairer than we found it; to build upon it cities of God in which the cry of needless pain shall cease; and to put the yoke of Christ upon our business life that it may serve and not destroy.

One Who Is Old in
Quest of Truth

PSALM 71:14-19

*O God, from my youth you have taught me, and I still
proclaim your wondrous deeds. So even to old age and
gray hairs, O God, do not forsake me, until I proclaim your
might to all the generations to come.* (NRSV)

It is always a splendid victory of the spirit over the body
when an old man or woman compels the brain to overcome the physiological inertia of age and receive new ideas
and convictions. In doing so, that person comes out of the
shelter of a system of thought which he or she has built in
a long life and which hitherto seemed complete and sufficient, and takes the staff in hand once more to go in quest
of the Holy Grail of truth. When a person of ripe years,
whose religious horizon was formerly bounded by routine
church work, soul-saving, and the premillennial hope, now
opens his or her heart to the social hope of the new age, we
may well feel the deepest reverence for such spiritual energy.
But we may also be sure that these old ones would not see
visions unless a new Pentecostal Spirit had been poured out
on all the disciples.

*Overcome our coldness and reserve that we may throw
ajar the gates of our hearts and keep open house this day.*

The Joy of Play

PROVERBS 15:13; 17:22

A cheerful heart is a good medicine. (NRSV)

The real joy of life is in its play. Play is anything we do for the joy and love of doing it, apart from any profit, compulsion, or sense of duty. It is the real living of life with the feeling of freedom and self-expression. Play is the business of childhood, and its continuation in later years is the prolongation of youth. Real civilization should increase the margin of time given to play . . . The killing of play means taking the life out of life.

When workers strive for leisure and health and a better wage, do thou grant their cause success, but teach them not to waste their gain on fleeting passions, but to use it in building fairer homes and a nobler life.

Fatal Attraction

MATTHEW 6:19-21, 24

Wherever your treasure is, your heart will be also.
You cannot serve God and money. (Goodspeed)

Jesus said that riches have so fatal an attraction over our mind that our heart is sure to be bound up with our wealth. As a consequence, the service of money and the service of God are mutually exclusive, and we must make our choice . . . Every proof that we love Mammon with all our heart and all our soul raises the presumption that we have lost the love of God and are merely going through the motions when we worship God. We can measure the general apostasy by noting the wonder and love that follow those who have even in some slight degree really turned their backs on money. People crowd around them like exiles around one who brings them news from home. We must change our economic system in order to preserve our conscience and our religious faith; we must renew and strengthen our religion in order to be able to change our economic system.

Behold the servants of Mammon, who rackrent the poor and make dear the space and air which thou hast made free; who paralyze the hand of justice by corruption and blind the eyes of the people by lies.

Too Much!

MARK 10:17-22

Jesus loved him as he looked at him.

The late Duke of Cambridge had a way of talking aloud to himself, even in church. One Sunday the lesson about Zacchaeus was being read, who gave away half of his goods to the poor. "Gad," said the Duke, "I don't mind subscribing, but half is too much." The rich young ruler was asked to give the whole and went away sorrowful. He wanted the goods, but the price staggered him. He missed his chance by not being game. He stood shivering on the shore and feared the plunge from which he would have come up in a tingle of life. He might have traveled day by day in the company of Jesus, with the Master's words in his memory, his eye on him, his friendship coaxing every good thing in the man's heart up and out. He might have become an apostle, one of the guiding spirits of the young Church, handling growing responsibilities, seeing the world, facing kings and mobs, tasting the fullness of life. Instead of that he probably lived and died as the richest man of his little Galilean town, carrying in a frozen heart the dead seed of a great life.

Grant that the strength which we shall draw from our daily bread may be put forth again for the common good, and that our life may return to humanity a full equivalent in useful work for the nourishment which we receive from the common store.

God Is the Great Joy

LAMENTATIONS 3:17-26

*The steadfast love of the LORD never ceases, his mercies
never come to an end; they are new every morning;
great is your faithfulness.* (NRSV)

The sacrifices demanded by a religious conversion always
seem sore and insuperable, but every religious person will
agree that after the great surrender is made, there is a radiant
joy that marks a great culmination of life. All the remaining
years are ennobled. God is the great joy. Whenever we have
touched the hem of his garment by some righteous action,
we get so much satisfaction that we can be well content
even if we get no further reward or recognition, or even if
we suffer hurt and persecution for it. Not the memory of
power wielded, not even the memory of love, is so sweet as
the consciousness that we once suffered for a great cause.

*O God, thou knowest how often we have resisted thee
and loved the easy ways of sin rather than the toilsome
gain of self-control and thy divine invitation of thy truth.
Visit not upon us the guilt of the past, for our forebears
have slain thy prophets. They silenced the voices that
spoke thine inward thought and quenched the light of
truth.*

The Joy of Prayer

PSALM 139:1-18

Where can I go from your spirit? Or where can I flee from your presence? If I take the wings of the morning and settle at the farthest limits of the sea, even there your hand shall lead me, and your right hand shall hold me fast. (NRSV)

There are many joys in life . . . but is any of them quite like the joy of prayer? Any one who has ever experienced it will always be haunted by homesickness for it. It surpasses other pleasures not only in degree, but in kind. It does not pall. It does not lash us on with the desire for a satisfaction which seems always just ahead and yet always eludes us. It is inexpressibly satisfying while it lasts; every renewal of it is good; there is always more ahead, and yet we are strangely content with what we have. It combines desire and satisfaction, progress and rest. There is a strange sweetness in a real prayer when you are conscious of touching God.

We feel our utter need of thee, thou great companion of our souls. Be thou the strength of our weakness, the wisdom of our foolishness, the triumph of our failures, the changeless unity in our changing days.

A Bible within the Bible

1 PETER 1:22-25
You have been born anew, not of perishable, but of imperishable seed, by the living, lasting word of God. For the grass fades, the flower falls, but the word of the Lord abides forever.

God's world is great; too great for a little mind like mine to hold. I have traveled over thousands of miles of it, but for the most part my memory holds only a blur of space and movement.

But there are a few places which my memory has made all my own. Way up on the Ox Tongue River is a high, straight fall, and above it a platform of rock. I lay there one night in the open, while the cool night wind moved the treetops, and watched the constellations march across the spaces between them. That place is mine by the emotions and prayers it inspired.

The world of the Bible, too, is a great world. I have wandered through it all, but I have never made it all my own. But some friendly hills and valleys in it are mine by right of experience. Some chapters have comforted me; some have made me homesick; some have braced me like a bugle call; and some always enlarge me within by a sense of unutterable fellowship with a great, quiet Power that pervades all things and fills me.

Such passages make up for each of us a Bible within the Bible, and the extent and variety of these claims we have staked out in it measure how much of the great Book has really entered into the substance of our life.

We thank thee for the voices that have interpreted thy will and summoned us to thy work.

The Little Chapter of Love

1 CORINTHIANS 13

Love will bear anything, believe anything, hope for anything, endure anything. Love will never die out. (Goodspeed)

The thirteenth chapter of Paul's first letter to the Corinthians . . . has gentled our resentful feelings and made us forgiving. By making us feel the worth of love, it has made us feel the worth of those we ought to love. The old psalm ascribes to the pilgrim saints of God the capacity to "pass through the valley of weeping" and leave it "a place of springs." This little chapter has done just that by its irrigation of affection and cleansed will.

Since we daily crave thy mercy on our weakness, help us now to show mercy to those who have this day grieved or angered us and to forgive them utterly.

The Revelation of God

JOHN 12:44-50

*Whoever believes in me, believes not in me but in him who
sent me; and whoever sees me, sees him who sent me. I have
come into the world as a light, so that no one who believes
in me may have to remain in darkness.* (Goodspeed)

The revelation of God in Christ is greater than the teachings
of Jesus. Christ did not receive revelations; he was the revelation. The prophets received communications from God,
and knew that they received them. To them it was the dis-
tinguishing mark of true prophets that they received communications from Jehovah, while the false prophets spoke
their own mind and fancies . . . Christ drew from the depths
of his own nature and consciousness. His words were but
expressions of himself. His vision of God and the kingdom
was not the ideal of a few hours of exaltation, but was one
with his life . . . He was one with his message. The Word of
the Lord came to Jeremiah; Christ was the Word of God.
The Word had become human nature. The prophet could
say at times, "Those who hear my words hear the words of
God"; Christ could say at all times, "Those who see me see
the Father."

*We lean on thee, thou great giver of life, and pray for
physical vigor and quiet strength. We call to thee, thou
fountain of light, to flood our minds with thy radiance
and to make all things clear and simple.*

The Higher Life

COLOSSIANS 3:1-4

Seek those things which are above, where Christ abides.
Set your heart on things above.

There is a realm superior to body and mind, a greatness that excels even intellectual genius. To do right is greater than to be strong. To be good is worthier than to be clever. The spiritual life is highest and its cultivation most important of all. The spirit outlasts the body and outlasts the mind. It shines in an old saint like the gleam of the sword in a wornout scabbard. It gives promise of a day of glorious unfolding like the bud of a flower in which the rosy tints of the corolla just show through the green leaves of the calyx. It is the one thing in life that lasts; the sifted grain of all our labor and weariness; the one thing that God will ask for.

Grant us, we pray thee, a heart wide open to all joy and beauty of this universe, and save our souls from being so steeped in care or so darkened by passion that we pass heedless and unseeing when even the thornbush by the wayside is aflame with the glory of God.

Tending the Spiritual Life

GALATIANS 5:16-26

But the harvest-fruit of the Spirit is love, joy, peace, long-suffering, kindness, goodness, fidelity, gentleness, and self-control. If we are living by the Spirit, let us also keep step in the Spirit.

The spiritual life needs cultivation, conscious and careful tending, for it is like a flower in sterile soil and under a hostile climate. Compare the powerful push of our sensuous impulses with the fragile growth of our God-ward aspirations. How alert we are when our selfishness spurs us, and how very feebly we stir when love or pity or unselfish love of right demands our action. Whether we have fallen and have been corrupted by ages of sin, as the Bible says, or whether we are slowly mounting from the purely animal life to the spiritual, as the doctrine of evolution asserts, in either case it remains true that the spiritual life is as yet very feeble in humanity. If it is to grow, it must not be left to the rude conflict with hostile forces of the flesh and the world, but must be consciously fostered.

O Christ, look with thy great sympathy on thy servants. Thou knowest the drain of our daily work and the limitations of our bodies. Thou knowest that we carry but a little candle of knowledge to guide the feet of the erring amid the mazes of modern life. Thou knowest that our longing for holiness of heart is frustrated by the drag of our earthliness and the weight of ancient sins.

My Old Christianity

ACTS 11:1-18

Who was I that I could withstand God?

Where does the social question come in? Where does the matter come in of saving the world? That was the real difficulty in my thought all the time—how to find a place, under the old religious conceptions, for this great task of changing the world and making it righteous; making it habitable; making it neighborly. Somehow I knew in my soul that that was God's work. Nobody could wrest that from me. Jesus Christ had spoken too plainly to my soul about that. I knew that he was on the side of righteousness, and on the side of his poor brother and sister. But where could I get it with my old Christianity—with my old religion?

O God, we pray thee for those who come after us, for our children, and the children of our friends, and for all the young lives that are marching up from the gates of birth, pure and eager, with the morning sunshine on their faces. We remember with a pang that these will live in the world we are making for them.

The New Life of Faith

ACTS 2:37-47

*They stedfastly continued in the teaching of the apostles,
and in the fellowship, in the breaking of the bread,
and in the prayers. Meanwhile the Lord kept adding
to them daily those that were being saved.*

Original Christianity was exceedingly simple; it was just a new life with God and a new life with others. Faith in Christ was a spiritual experience. Those who believed in him felt a new spirit, a Holy Spirit, living in their hearts, inspiring their prayers and testimonies, melting away their selfishness, emboldening them to heroism. Paul called that new life "faith." That word with him does not merely mean an intellectual belief. It is a kind of algebraic symbol expressing the inner religious experience and life in Christ.

*O baptize thy church afresh in the life-giving spirit of
Jesus! Grant her a new birth, though it be with the travail
of repentance and humiliation.*

A Faith to Cover the Whole

1 CORINTHIANS 10:31–11:1

You are to do it all for the glory of God.

A real religion always wants unity. It wants to bring the whole world into one great conception that can inspire and fill the soul. It sees one God, it wants one world, it wants one redemption. That is faith. No faith is really complete that cuts life up into sections and applies on to a little bit of it. We want faith always as a whole thing.

And so my desire was always for faith that would cover my whole life.

O thou strong Father of all nations, draw all thy great family together with an increasing sense of our common blood and destiny, that peace may come on earth at last, and thy sun may shed its light rejoicing on a holy community of peoples.

Fellowship of Saints

LUKE 24:13-35

Then they began to tell what happened on the road, and Jesus was known to them when he broke the bread.

There is a dry atmosphere of unbelief in the world, in its conversation, its aims, its literature. It saps our faith. People live as if there is no God. To counter that we must associate with those to whom God is a living reality. We can associate with men and women of God in past ages by reading their thoughts in the Bible or in the books of devotion they have left us. We can associate with people who are distinctively spiritual in our acquaintance and encourage them to talk to us of the deeper experiences of their faith. There is wonderful strength in such fellowship of the saints.

We thank thee for those who share our higher life, the comrades of our better self, in whose companionship we break the mystic bread of life and feel the glow of thy wonderful presence.

So Diverse Yet the Same

1 CORINTHIANS 12:4-13

Now there are varieties of gifts, but the same Spirit;
there are various forms of service, and the same Lord; and
varieties of work, and the same God, who works in all.

Religion has taken a great variety of forms in the various Christian bodies. Take a solemn mass in a Roman Catholic cathedral, with the dim religious light, the swelling music, the candles, the trooping of the priests and acolytes, the wafting of the incense, the tinkle of the bell, the prostration of the people as the wafer is miraculously transformed into the very body of the Lord. Take on the other hand a little experience meeting in a country church where one simple soul after the other arises to tell in rude words of its dealings with God. How far apart they are! And yet it is only fair to believe that all Christian bodies aim at the same thing: to bring the human soul into saving contact with God through Christ and to secure for it the knowledge and power of a holy life. Let us rejoice that we are all one in that fundamental aim.

Brood over our assemblies with thy Holy Spirit. Give us vision beyond the range of worldly prudence, and by thy wisdom make us wise, lest all our planning be futile. If difficulties confront us, give us the courageous faith that bids the mountains melt away. Smite a pathway even across the impassable sea for thy people.

Second-hand Religion

PSALM 34

This poor soul cried, and was heard by the LORD, and was saved from every trouble. O taste and see that the LORD is good. (NRSV)

The great mass of people take their religion at second hand. Some strong religious soul in the past has had a real experience with God and tells others about it; they believe it and then take their belief in that experience as a substitute for having any such experience themselves . . . The thoughts and experiences of others are invaluable to us because they enrich and broaden our own, but in religion nothing will take the place of personal experience [of the soul with God].

Intellectual statements of belief are useful if they are the outgrowth of personal experience; if not, they are likely to be a harmful substitute for experience.

Now consider how great a thing it is for a church body to assert that a person may and must come into direct personal relations with God, and to adapt all its church life to create such direct and spiritual experiences in people. I have met people in other churches who not only have no such experience themselves, but they doubt if anybody can have it. It seems presumption to them for someone to assert that he or she knows to have received pardon from God and is living in conscious fellowship with God. Yet what is all the apparatus of church life good for if it does not help people to that experience?

O Master, amidst our failures we cast ourselves upon thee in humility and contrition. We need new light and a new message. We need the leaping fire and joy of a new conviction, and thou alone canst give it.

Being and Doing

MATTHEW 12:33-37

By its fruit the tree is known.

Character is formed by action, but after it is formed, it determines action. What someone says and does, that one becomes; and what that one becomes, he or she says and does. An honest and clear-minded person instinctively does what is kind and honorable. But when a person for years has gone for profit and selfish power, you can trust the person as a general thing to do what is underhanded and mean. Since selfish ability elbows its way to controlling positions in business, politics, and society, the character reactions of such people are a force with which the kingdom of God must reckon. They are the personal equipment of the kingdom of evil, and the more respectable, well-dressed, and clever they are, the worse it is.

O God, thou great governor of all the world, we pray thee for all who hold public office and power, for the life, the welfare, and the virtue of the people are in their hands to make or to mar. Strengthen the sense of duty in our political life. Grant that the servants of the state may feel ever more deeply that any diversion of their public powers for private ends is a betrayal of their country.

In Times of Doubt

PSALM 91

*When they call to me, I will answer them; I will be with them
in trouble, I will rescue them and honor them.* (NRSV)

When we insist on repentance from sin and submission to
the will of God, that is a religious experience directly leading to a higher moral life. Such religion lends the most powerful reinforcement to ethical duty and is of high service to
the common life of humanity.

We can see how profoundly important such a direct
experience of God is from the fact that in times of doubt
it is often the only thing that remains unshaken. Many a
person has felt intellectual beliefs crumbling away, and yet
faith in God weathered the storm like a granite cliff. When
arguments went to pieces, that person could still say: "But
I know that God made a new person of me; the experience
I had in years gone by is just as certain to me as that I am
alive." And on that basis he or she was able to build up a
wider faith. A church that helps people to personal experience of religion, therefore helps them to the most essential
and abiding thing in the moral and spiritual life.

*O thou whose light is about me and within me and to
whom all things are present, help me this day to keep my
life pure in thy sight. If any dear heart has staked its life
and hopes on my love and loyalty, I beseech thee that its
joy and strength may never wither through my forgetfulness or guilt. O God, make me pure and a helper to the
weak.*

Go into That Inner Solitude

1 KINGS 19:11-12

*Not in the wind, not in the earthquake, not in the fire;
and after the fire a sound of sheer silence.* (NRSV)

Baptists in all their church life emphasize the necessity of personal experience with God and thus confront the soul with God to work out its spiritual salvation. As Moses or Elijah or John the Baptist met God alone amid the lonely crags of the desert, so we want every person to go into that inner solitude of one's own soul where no one can follow, to hear the still small voice of the Eternal and to settle the past and the future with the great Spirit of the spirit.

Hush all spirit of contention and self-will. Make us peaceful through love and through the unity of our desire.

Above All Else

GALATIANS 2:20

It is Christ who is living in me.

First of all and above everything comes evangelical Christianity. And what do I mean by that? I mean by that, not any particular type of doctrine, but the extension of faith in the crucified and risen Christ, who imparts his Spirit to those who believe in him, and thereby redeems them from the dominion of the flesh and the world and their corruption, and transforms them into spiritual beings, conformed to his likeness and partaking of his life. That is the primary aim of Christian missions, first in the order of importance, first in the order of time.

O Jesus, thou master of all who are both strong and pure, take our weak and passionate hearts under thy control, that when the dusk settles upon our life, we may go to our long rest with no pang of shame, and may enter into the blessedness of seeing God.

Instructions in Case of My Death, March 1918

REVELATION 14:12-13

Blessed are the dead that die in the Lord from henceforth!
Yea, says the Spirit, that they may rest from their labors,
for their deeds do follow them.

I leave my love to those of my friends whose souls have never grown dark against me, I forgive the others and hate no one. For my errors and weaknesses, I hope to be forgiven by my fellows. I had long prayed God not to let me be stranded in a lonesome and useless old age, and if this is the meaning of my present illness, I shall take it as a loving mercy of God toward this servant. Since 1914 the world is full of hate, and I cannot expect to be happy again in my lifetime. I had hoped to write several books which had been in my mind, but doubtless others can do the work better. The only pang is to part from my loved ones, and no longer to be able to stand by them and smooth their way. For the rest I go gladly, for I have carried a heavy handicap for thirty years and have worked hard.

We praise thee that to us Death is no more an enemy but thy great angel and our friend, who alone can open for some of us the prison-house of pain and misery and set our feet in the roomy spaces of a larger life. Thou art the father of our spirits; from thee we have come; to thee we go. We rejoice that in the hours of our purer vision, when the pulse-throb of thine eternity is strong within us, we know that no pang of mortality can reach our unconquerable soul, and that for those who abide in thee death is but the gateway to life eternal. Into thy hands we commend our spirit.

Walter Rauschenbusch died on July 25, 1918.

The Outward Journey

Serve God
Aid the Kingdom
Bless Humanity

"A Christlike life
without putting forth Christlike words and deeds
is a delusion.
And a putting forth of Christlike words and deeds
without checking evil and extending God's reign
is inconceivable."

Walter Rauschenbusch
"The Righteousness of the Kingdom"
Early 1890s

Now the God of all hope fill you with all joy and peace
in believing, that you may be overflowing with hope in the
power of the Holy Spirit. (Romans 15:13)

The Inward and the Outward

MATTHEW 7:15-23

*A good tree cannot bear bad fruit; neither can
a worthless tree bear good fruit.*

By his entire life, Jesus showed that he regarded the spiritual nature of human beings, the religious and moral element, as the core of the individual life and the real formative force in the life of society.

But while Jesus began his work on the inward and spiritual side of human life, he did not propose to let it end there . . . There was nothing that Jesus resented so much as an attempt to divorce the inward from the outward; to be saying, "Lord, Lord!" and then not to obey him; to parade as a good tree and yet bring no fruit or bitter fruit.

We invoke thy grace and wisdom, O Lord, upon all those of good will who employ and control the labor of others. When they are tempted to follow the ruthless ways of others, and to sacrifice human health and life for profit, do thou strengthen their will in the hour of need, and bring to naught the counsels of the heartless.

The Kingdom Touches Everything

GALATIANS 6:14-15

Neither circumcision nor the want of it is of any importance, but only a new creation. (Goodspeed)

The idea of the kingdom of God was something so big that absolutely nothing that interested me was excluded from it. Was it a matter of personal religion? Why the kingdom of God begins with that! The powers of the kingdom of God well up in the individual soul; that is where they are born and that is where the starting point must necessarily be. Was it a matter of world-wide missions? Why that is the kingdom of God, isn't it—carrying it out to the boundaries of the earth. Was it a matter of getting justice for workers? Is not justice part of the kingdom of God? Does not the kingdom of God consist in this—that God's will shall be done on earth, even as it is done in heaven? And so whatever I touched, there was the kingdom of God. That was the brilliance, the splendor of that conception—it touches everything with religion. It carries God into everything that you do.

O God, thou mightiest worker of the universe, source of all strength and author of all unity, we pray thee for the workers of the nation. Teach them to keep step in a steady onward march, and in their own way to fulfill the law of Christ by bearing the common burdens.

Least Wanting to Hear

LUKE 4:16-30

When they heard these words of Jesus, those in the synagogue were filled with fury; they rose, hurried him outside the town, and brought him to the brow of the hill on which their city was built, intending to cast him down headlong. But Jesus, passing through the midst of them, took his departure.

The Church has the prophetic office in humanity. Because it is in contact with God, its conscience quickened, its ethical discernment clarified, its moral courage and energy strengthened, it is to be the teacher of society. It is to discern injustice where it is hidden to others by force of habit. It is to hear the sob of pain in the outcast classes whom others pass unheeded. It is to detect the sallow face of tyranny hiding behind the mask of patriotism and benevolence. Who is fit to do this if the Church is not? It is exactly this prophetic office the Church is to fulfill.

When I am asked to speak anywhere, I always ask myself, "What is there that these people ought to hear *that they least like to hear?*" and then speak on that!

If others speak well of us, may we not be puffed up; if they slight us, may we not be cast down; remembering the words of our Master who bade us rejoice when people speak evil against us and tremble if any speak well, that so we may have evidence that we are still soldiers of God.

Sin of Omission

JAMES 4:13-17

*To those who know how to do right and do not do it,
to them it is sin.*

When God gave the Spirit to few, God called few to his service. Now that God offers his Spirit to all, God calls all to his work. It is a holy duty and we shirk it at our peril. If even a single good action, which we knew how to do and which we left undone, is counted as sin, how much more will God so consider a lifetime of service which we knew was asked for and which we refused? I think God will more easily pardon many a hot sin of commission, than that cool, life-long, damning sin of omission.

May there be nothing in this day's work of which we shall be ashamed when the sun has set, nor in the eventide of our life when our task is done and we go to our long home to meet thy face.

The Privilege of Service

MATTHEW 20:25-28

Whoever wants to be great among you must be your servant.
(Goodspeed)

A life of service is a holy duty. Yes, and a blessed privilege too. How swiftly life spins away! And sometimes as I listen to the racing of the years, I feel a terrible catch of the heart, not at the coming of death, but at the passing of life. So much to be done, and as yet so little accomplished. I want to work, to serve in the redemption of the world from wrong, to help my Master save humanity. It is a glory, a privilege, and I want much of it. This life can be so full, so noble, so blessed to us, so useful to others. And so often it is empty, vapid, trivial, discontented, useless. Which is the real privilege, to serve or to idle? Which is the real burden, to live for self or to live for the kingdom of God?

As we look across the vast field of our work, O Master, we feel the challenge of thy call and turn to thee for strength. So much to do for thee, and so little wherewith to do it.

All Are Called

1 PETER 4:10-11

Whatever the gifts which each has received, use them for one another, as good stewards of the manifold grace of God.

In this age of the democracy of the Holy Spirit, the call to service is not restricted to a few, not to the ministry, not even to those who have the gift of speech. In the great field of the kingdom, here is a duty for all: for those with the gift of speech, and those with the gift of action; for the burning mind and for the gentle cooling hand; for the leader of men and women and the trainer of little children. All are called; all have the duty; all have the privilege; all may have the equipment . . . Look down the future and see the tongues of fire leaping from heart to heart, enlisting in holy ministry . . . till all hands are busy in building the spiritual temple of God, and all hearts repeat in unison as the dominant note of their lives: "Thy will be done on earth."

May we not be so wholly of one mind with the life that now is that the world can fully approve us, but may we speak the higher truth and live the purer righteousness which thou hast revealed to us.

The Question to Ask Yourself

MATTHEW 6:25-33

*Continue to seek first God's kingdom and righteousness,
and all these things shall be added to you.*

Let each of us ask ourselves the question: In what way does my daily work serve the kingdom of God? If we cannot find an answer, let us consider if our conception of the kingdom of God is as wide as the purposes of God would have it. If we cannot answer the question yet, let us consult others. And if after all this we cannot see that our daily work in any sense aids the kingdom, serves God, and blesses humanity, but if it is merely fit to put bread and cake into our stomachs, let us get out of it, for in that line of business we can never obey one of the fundamental principles of Christ's teaching: "Seek ye first the kingdom of God."

*Accept every right intention however brokenly fulfilled,
but grant that ere our life is done we may under thy
tuition become true master workers, who know the art
of a just and valiant life.*

I Could Not Keep Silent

JEREMIAH 20:7-9

*Within me there is something like a burning fire
shut up in my bones.* (NRSV)

In my efforts to secure more freedom and justice for men and women I acted under religious impulses. I realized that God hates injustices and that I would be quenching the life of God within me if I kept silent with all this social iniquity around me.

It must be plain to any thoughtful observer that immense numbers of people are turning away from traditional religion, not because they have lapsed into sin, but because they have become modernized in their knowledge and points of view. The real religious leaders of this generation must face the problem how they can give to modern people the inestimable boon of experiencing God as a joy and a power and of living in God as their forebears did. I claim that social Christianity is by all tokens the great highway by which this present generation can come to God.

O Lord, thou art the eternal order of the universe. Our human laws at best are but an approximation of thine immutable law, and if our institutions are to stand, they must rest on justice, for only justice can endure.

Show Me What to Do

JAMES 1:5-8

*Ask God who gives generously to everyone, and
God will give it to you. (Goodspeed)*

The fibers of the muscles grow by use. So does the moral and religious fiber. Serve God and it will become easy to serve God. Lend a hand, and the hand you lent will come back suppler and stronger. If there is any one of my readers who wants to work, but doesn't know what to work at, let me present a rule which I think is quite infallible. Let my readers ask God straightforwardly to show them what God wants them to do, and I think I can promise them that they will stumble over tasks so thick that they will hardly have time to pick them all up.

Grant us of thy mercy a valiant heart, that we may tread the road with head uplifted and a smiling face. May we do our work to the last with a wholesome joy, and love our loves with an added tenderness because the days of love are short.

Love at the Center

LUKE 6:27-38

But I tell you who hear me, love your enemies,
treat those who hate you well, bless those who curse you,
pray for those who abuse you. You will be children
of the Most High, for he is kind even to the ungrateful and
the wicked. You must be merciful, just as your Father is.
(Goodspeed)

Now Jesus with incomparable spiritual energy set love into the center of religion. He drove home the duty of love with words so mighty that we can never again forget them. He embodied the principle of love in the undying charm and youthful strength of his own life in such a way as to exert an assimilating compulsion over more lives than we can number. He was conscious of God as a sunny and loveable presence and he taught his friends to think of God as a father who loved them unselfishly and wanted nothing from them except love. This conception of God was reinforced when people saw in the cross the great declaration of the redemptive love of God.

O God, we who are bound together in the tender ties of love pray thee for a day of unclouded love. May no passing irritation rob us of our joy in one another.

Pioneers of the Kingdom of God

EPHESIANS 4:13-16

Holding the truth in love we shall grow up in every part into him who is our Head, even Christ. From him the whole body makes continual growth so as to build itself up in love.

Christianity clearly needs active personal agents who will incarnate its vitalities, propagate its principles, liberate its underdeveloped forces, purify its doctrine, and extend the sway of its faith in love over new realms of social life. Dare we be such men and women? Dare we be Christians? Those who take up the propaganda of love and substitute freedom and fraternity for coercion and class differences in social life are the pioneers of the kingdom of God, for the reign of the God of love will be fulfilled in a life of humanity organized on the basis of solidarity and love.

O Thou Great Lover of us all, all the tender beauty of our human loves is the reflected radiance of thy loving kindness, like the moonlight from the sunlight, and testifies to the eternal passion that kindled it.

Essence of Baptist Faith

JOHN 9:1-41

One thing I do know, that once I was blind,
and now I can see.

Baptists, in tying to the New Testament, have hitched their chariot to a star, and they will have to keep moving.

I am a Baptist because in our church life we have a minimum of emphasis on ritual and creed, and a maximum of emphasis on spiritual experience, and the more I study the history of religion, the more I see how great and fruitful such a position is.

Many [Baptists] do not even realize that that is the essence of our Baptist faith. We have some who insist on immersion in a purely legal and ritualistic spirit. We have others who would be only too glad if we had an ironclad Baptist creed with a thousand points that they may might insist on it . . . But our Baptist faith, like our American political constitution, is founded on great principles, and even if some misuse it or misunderstand it, or are inwardly traitors to it, its greatness lifts others up to it. Baptists uphold Baptist principles; and Baptist principles in turn lift up Baptists.

We bless thee that we are set amidst thine rich kindred life with its mysterious power to quicken and uplift.

The Spirit of True Christianity

PHILIPPIANS 4:4-9

Rejoice in the Lord alway, and again will I say, rejoice!

In our common worship we shall come closest to the spirit of true Christianity if every act is full of joy in God and fellowship with God, love for one another, hatred of all evil, and an honest desire to live a right life in the sight of Christ. Our worship should eliminate as far as possible all selfish greed and all untrue and unworthy ideas of God. It should clear our conception of the right life by instructing our moral nature; it should give our will strong, steady, lasting impulses toward righteous action; and it should breed and foster habits of reverence and the faculty of adoration.

Make us, we pray thee, friends of all the world. Save us from blighting the fresh flower of any heart by the flare of sudden anger or secret hate. May we not bruise the rightful self-respect of any by contempt or malice. Help us to cheer the suffering by our sympathy, to freshen the drooping by our hopefulness, and to strengthen in all the wholesome sense of worth and the joy of life.

Perpetual Reformation for the Church

ACTS 6:1-7

And the word of the Lord continued to spread.

The Bible is alive. And such a life in it! A unique and gifted nation, with a lofty conception of God and a thrilling faith in God, preserves the thoughts of its most daring thinkers, its prophets and revolutionists, its poets and religious historians, and the whole collection throbs with the living breath of God—if only we have a mind to respond. And then comes the Highest One of all, the Son of God and the King of Humanity, and his life and thought are preserved in artless books, and the powerful impulse which he gives to human souls records itself in a series of letters and tracts, and these are added to the old Bible of the Jewish people as the New Bible of the Christian people.

These books are the deposit of the purest and freshest form of Christianity. The New Testament has been the conscience in the heart of the church, always warning and recalling it from its sinful wanderings. It is still calling us up higher today, beyond traditional Christianity to the religion of Christ. In the New Testament lies the power to perpetual reformation for the Church.

O thou Eternal One, we adore thee who in all ages hast been the great companion and teacher of humankind; for thou hast lifted us from the depths, and hast made us to share in thy conscious intelligence and thy will that makes for righteousness and love.

Let the Bible's Light Break Forth

MATTHEW 15:1-9

You make void the word of God by your tradition!

We have paralyzed the Bible by turning it into a lawbook and a collection of proof texts. We have often refused to comprehend the larger sweep of history in it. We have fussed about trifles in it and have missed the greatest things. But my faith is that the old veil of Moses will yet be taken away from the Bible and its full light will break forth.

Baptists have undertaken to learn what the Bible can tell them and to guide their life thereby. This is to me a satisfactory adjustment between the two great principles of freedom and authority; between the initiative of the individual and the authority of the church; between faithfulness to the past and obedience to the call of the future.

Inspire the ministry of thy Church with dauntless courage to face the vast needs of the future. Free us from all entanglements that have hushed our voice and bound our action.

Dangerous Religion

2 CORINTHIANS 6:1-13

My heart is wide open to you.
I pray, let your hearts also be wide open to me.

Personal sanctification must serve the kingdom of God. Any mystic experience which makes our fellow human beings less real and daily labor less noble is dangerous religion. A religious experience is not Christian unless it binds us closer to others and commits us more deeply to the kingdom of God. To be afraid of hell and desirous of a life without pain or trouble in heaven was not in itself Christian. It was self-interest on a higher level. As long as people are wholly intent on their own destiny, they do not necessarily emerge from selfishness. It only changes its form. A Christian regeneration must have an outlook toward humanity and result in a higher social consciousness.

May Christ's spirit of duty and service ennoble all we do. Uphold us by the consciousness that our work is useful work and a blessing to all.

The Fellowship of Redemptive Love

1 PETER 1:3-9

*For a brief moment you have suffered many hardships.
These are in order that the test of your faith may redound to
praise and glory and honor, at the revelation of Jesus Christ.*

Those who take social Christianity at all seriously will certainly encounter opposition and be bruised somehow. Such an experience will throw them back on the comforts of God and make their prayers more than words. When they bear on their own body and soul the marks of the Lord Jesus, the cross will be more than a doctrine to them. It will be a bond uniting them with Christ in the fellowship of redemptive love.

If the evil that is threatened turns to smite us and if we must learn the dark malignity of sinful power, comfort us by the thought that thus we are bearing in our body the marks of Jesus, and that only those who share in his free sacrifice shall feel the plentitude of thy life.

What God Wants

AMOS 5:21-24

*I hate, I despise your festivals; I take no delight in
your solemn assemblies. Take away from me the noise
of your songs. But let justice roll down like waters, and
righteousness like an ever-flowing stream.* (NRSV)

The fundamental conviction of the prophets . . . was the conviction that God demands righteousness and demands nothing but righteousness. The prophets insisted on a right life as
the true worship of God. Morality to them was not merely
a prerequisite of effective ceremonial worship. They brushed
sacrificial ritual aside altogether as trifling compared with
righteousness, nay, as a harmful substitute and a hindrance
for ethical religion . . . What God wanted was a right life and
the righting of social wrongs . . . They said less about the pure
heart for the individual than of just institutions for the nation.
The twin-evil against which the prophets launched the condemnation of Jehovah was injustice and oppression . . . The
morality which they had in mind was not the private morality
of detached pious souls but the social morality of the nation.

*We praise thee, Almighty God, for thine elect, the proph-
ets and martyrs of humanity, who gave their thoughts and
prayers and agonies for the truth of God and the freedom
of people. We praise thee that amid loneliness and the contempt of others, in poverty and imprisonment, when they
were condemned by the laws of the mighty and buffeted
on the scaffold, thou didst uphold them by thy Spirit in
loyalty to thy holy cause.*

The Sympathies of Jesus

MATTHEW 11:2-5

Are you the Coming One, or are we to look for someone else?

As with the Old Testament prophets, the fundamental sympathies of Jesus were with the poor and oppressed. In the glad opening days of his preaching in Galilee, when he wanted to unfold his program, he turned to the passage of Isaiah where the prophet proclaimed good tidings to the poor, release to the captives, liberty to the bruised, and the acceptable year of the Lord for all. Now, said Jesus, that is to be fulfilled. To John in prison, he offered as proof that the Messiah had really come, that the helpless were receiving help, and the poor were listening to glad news. The Church has used the miracles of Jesus for theological purposes as evidence of his divine mission. According to the Synoptic gospels, Jesus himself flatly refused to furnish them for such a purpose to the contemporary theologians. His healing power was for social help, for the alleviation of human suffering.

For the oppression of the poor and the sighing of the needy, now do thou arise, O Lord; for because thou art love, and tender as a mother to the weak, therefore thou art the great hater of iniquity and thy doom is upon those who grow rich on the poverty of the people.

Revolution and Reversal

LUKE 1:47-55

He has routed the proud-minded, He has dethroned the [powerful] and exalted the poor, He has satisfied the hungry with good things, and sent the rich away empty-handed. (Goodspeed)

There was a revolutionary consciousness in Jesus; not, of course, in the common use of the word "revolutionary," which connects it with violence and bloodshed. But Jesus knew that he had come to kindle a fire on earth. Much as he loved peace, he knew that the actual result of his work would be not peace but the sword. His mother in her song had recognized in her own experience the settled custom of God to "put down the proud and exalt them of low degree," to "fill the hungry with good things and to send the rich empty away." The son of Mary expected a great reversal of values. The first would be last and the last would be first . . . This revolutionary note runs even through the beatitudes where we should least expect it. The point of them is that henceforth those were to be blessed whom the world had not blessed, for the kingdom of God would reverse their relative standing. Now the poor and the hungry and the sad were to be satisfied and comforted; the meek who had been shouldered aside by the ruthless would get their chance to inherit the earth, and conflict and persecution would be inevitable in the process.

Change us by the power of thy saving grace from sources of evil into forces for good, that with all our strength we may fight the wrongs we have aided, and aid the right we have clogged.

Churchly Christianity

LUKE 11:37-44

Inside you are full of greed and wickedness. You fools!
Give your inmost life as charity, and you will
immediately find everything clean. (Goodspeed)

One of the profoundest changes in the history of Christianity took place when the simple groups of Christian believers, who were bound together in intimate social life by the same faith and hope, were transformed into a firmly organized, authoritative, and international ecclesiastical organization. Correct doctrine came to be essential to salvation . . . Perhaps the most distinctive characteristic of Christianity down to our own time has been its churchliness . . .

Christian morality finds its highest dignity and its constant corrective in making the kingdom of God the supreme aim to which all minor aims must contribute and from which they gain their moral quality. The Church substituted itself for the kingdom of God . . . The more churchly Christianity is, the more will the Church be the only sphere of really Christian activity . . . The rest is secular . . . it is not religious and holy.

When we compare thy Church with all other human institutions, we rejoice, for there is none like her. But when we judge her by the mind of the Master, we bow in pity and contrition.

The Church Is an Agent, Not an End

JOHN 17:13-19

As thou hast sent me into the world, even so
I also have sent them into the world.

In making historical criticisms on ecclesiasticism, I do not belittle the immense value and importance of Christian churches. Religion demands social expression like all other great human impulses. Without an organization to proclaim it, to teach it, to stimulate it, the religious life would probably be greatly weakened in the best, and in many would be powerless and unknown. The mischief begins when the Church makes herself the end. She does not exist for her own sake; she is simply a working organization to create the Christian life in individuals and the kingdom of God in human society. She is an agent with large powers, and like all other agents she is constantly tempted to use her powers for herself.

Her history is the story of how she fell by rising, and rose by falling. No one who loves her can serve her better than by bringing home to her that by seeking her life she loses it, and that when she loses her life to serve the kingdom of God she will gain it.

Bestow upon thy Church a more imperious responsiveness to duty, a swifter compassion with suffering, and an utter loyalty to the will of God.

Social Transformation Now

JOHN 5:1-17

My Father has continued working until now,
and I am working, too.

It is true that any regeneration of society can come only through the act of God and the presence of Christ; but God is now acting, and Christ is now here. To assert that means not less faith, but more. It is true that any effort at social regeneration is dogged by perpetual relapses and doomed forever to fall short of its aim. But the same is true of our personal efforts to live a Christlike life; it is true, also, of every local church, and of the history of the Church at large. Whatever argument would demand the postponement of social regeneration to a future era will equally demand the postponement of personal holiness to a future life. We must have the faith of the apostolic Church in the triumph of Christ over the kingdoms of the world, plus the knowledge which nineteen centuries of history have given to us. Unless we add that knowledge, the faith of the apostles becomes our unbelief.

We pray thee for those who amid all the knowledge of our day are still without knowledge; for those who hear not the sighs of the children that toil, nor the sobs of such as are wounded because others have made haste to be rich; for those that struggle vainly against poverty and vice. Arouse them, we beseech thee, from their selfish comfort and grant them the grace of social repentance.

Know the Devil

PHILIPPIANS 3:7-11

In very truth I count all things but loss compared to the excellence of the knowledge of Christ Jesus my Lord. For his sake I have suffered the loss of all things, and esteem them but refuse that I may gain Christ, and be found in him.

Evangelicalism prides itself on its emphasis on sin and the need of conversion, yet some of those trained in its teachings do not seem to know the devil when they meet him on the street. The most devastating sins of our age do not look like sins to them. They may have been converted from the world, but they contentedly make their money in the common ways of the world. Social Christianity involves a more trenchant kind of conversion and more effective means of grace. Those who get the spiritual ideals of social Christianity are really set at odds with "the world" and enlisted in a lifelong fight with organized evil. But no one who casts out devils is against Christ. To fight evil involves a constant affirmation of holiness and hardens the muscles of Christian character better than any religious gymnasium work. To very many Christians of the old type the cross of Christ meant only an expedient in the scheme of redemption, not a law of life for themselves. One can be an exponent of "the higher life" and never suffer any persecution whatever from the powers that control our sin-ridden social life.

If we must suffer loss, and drink of the bitter pool of misunderstanding and scorn, uphold us by thy Spirit in steadfastness and joy because we are found worthy to share in the work and the reward of Jesus and all the saints.

What Keeps Us Growing

2 THESSALONIANS 1:3-5

I ought always to thank God for you as is fitting because of the abundant growth of your faith and of the overflowing love with which every one of you is filled toward one another.

Dead religion narrows our freedom, contracts our horizon, limits our sympathies, and dwarfs our stature. Live religion brings a sense of emancipation, the exhilaration of spiritual health, a tenderer affection for all living things, widening thoughts and aims, and a sure conviction of the reality and righteousness of God. Devotion to the reign of God on earth will do that for a person and will do it continuously. A self-centered religion reaches the dead line soon. On the contrary, when our prime object is not our soul, but the kingdom of God, we have set our hands to a task that will never end and will always expand. It will make ever larger demands on our intellect, our sympathy, and our practical efficiency. It will work us to the last ounce of our strength. But it will keep us growing.

Bid thy Church cease from seeking her own life, lest she lose it. Make her valiant to give up her life to humanity, that like her crucified Lord she may mount by the path of the cross to a higher glory.

Confronting the Causes of Misery

EPHESIANS 6:10-18

Let your hearts be strengthened in the Lord, and in the power of his might. For our wrestling is not against flesh and blood, but against the despotisms, the empires, the rulers of this present darkness, the spirit-hosts of evil in the heavenly realm.

Any social work that deals with the causes of misery involves fighting, for the causes of misery are never only in the people who are miserable. They are chiefly in those who profit by their misery. The word redemption means literally emancipation and liberation from slavery. It involves making the exploiters quit exploiting. But if you try to make them stop, they will strike back and hurt you.

Behold the servants of Mammon, who defy thee and drain their fellows for gain; who grind down the strength of the workers by merciless toil and fling them aside when they are mangled and worn.

Goodness That Wakes Up the Devil

COLOSSIANS 1:24-29

I am now rejoicing in my sufferings on your behalf; and I am filling up in my own body what is yet lacking of the sufferings of Christ in behalf of the church, his Body.

For ages the cross of Christ has stood at the center of Christian theology. But many good people who are loud in their insistence on the cross as the only means of salvation have apparently never had any experience of the pain of the cross. They do not "bear the marks of the Lord Jesus." There are no scars on them anywhere. Their religion has served to make them respected. Everyone likes them for their goodness. But their goodness was never so good that it waked up the devil. They never antagonized profitable sin; so they never got hurt.

Help us in patience to carry forward the eternal cross of thy Christ, counting it joy if we, too, are sown as grains of wheat in the furrows of the world, for only by the agony of the righteous comes redemption.

Poor Hypocrites of Infidelity

PHILIPPIANS 1:27-30

For you have been granted the privilege not only of trusting in Christ but of suffering for him. (Goodspeed)

The kind of social work that deals with the causes of misery is today almost the only form of Christian work that involves the risk of persecution. Thereby it opens to us a living experience of the cross of Christ and a fellow-feeling with all his followers of the Church Militant, which has moved down the centuries in a thin red line, but to which the Church Dormant owes all it enjoys of the higher life. Such social work throws us back in loneliness on God whom we find near. Never let those who suffer unselfishly for the cause of truth or justice or liberty say that they are not religious or a Christian. Their life belies their professions. They are poor hypocrites of infidelity.

May we never bring upon us the blood of all the righteous by renewing the spirit of those who persecuted them in the past. Grant us rather that we, too, may be counted in the chosen band of those who have given their life as a ransom for many.

Service as a Path to God

EPHESIANS 6:23-24

*Peace to the brothers and sisters and love, with faith
from God our Father and the Lord Jesus Christ.*

To love others is an avenue to the living experience of God.
We should expect that those who are engaged in social work
with a really loving spirit will find religion growing in them.

This is one of the tests of our social work, Is it distilling
wonder and reverence, tenderness and awe in us? Has our
work for others quickened and deepened our sense of God?
If it has not, then it has not done much for us, and it is ques-
tionable if it has done anything lasting for others.

On the other hand if our work for others is earning us
the tremendous perquisite of a living knowledge of God,
let us be thankful and go ahead. It is worth a lifetime to get
that.

*Lift our human friendships to the level of spiritual com-
panionship. May we realize thee as the eternal bond of
our unity. Shine upon us from the faces of thy servants,
thou all-pervading beauty, that in loving them we may be
praising thee.*

Fellowship through Service

PHILIPPIANS 2:12-18

Shine like stars in a dark world.

"Sanctification," according to almost any definition, is the continuation of that process of spiritual education and transformation, by which a human personality becomes a willing organ of the spirit of Christ. Those who believe in the social gospel can share in any methods for the cultivation of the spiritual life, if only they have an ethical outcome. Sanctification is through increased fellowship with God and others. But fellowship is impossible without an exchange of service.

Grant us an unerring instinct for what is right and true, and a swift sympathy to divine those who truly love and serve thy people.

The Test for the Church

MARK 3:1-5

Is it lawful to do good on the Sabbath Day, or to do harm?
to save a life, or to destroy it? They were silent.

Jesus criticized the most earnest religious people of his day because their religion harmed people instead of helping them. It was unsocial, or anti-social.

The spiritual center on which Jesus took his stand and from which he judged all things was the kingdom of God, the perfect social order. Even the ordinances of religion must justify themselves by making an effective contribution to the kingdom of God. The Sabbath was made for humankind, and its observance must meet the test of service to the welfare of humankind. It must function wholesomely. The candle must give light, or what is the use of it? The salt must be salty and preserve from decay, or it will be thrown out and trodden under foot. If the fig-tree bears no fruit, why is it allowed to use up space and crowd better plants off the soil? This, then, is Christ's test in matters of institutional religion. The Church and all its doings must serve the kingdom of God.

O Christ, thou hast bidden us pray for the coming of thy Father's kingdom, in which God's righteous will shall be done on earth. We have treasured thy words, but we have forgotten their meaning, and thy great hope has grown dim in thy Church.

The Irrepressible Conflict

MATTHEW 10:34-39

No one who will not take up the cross and follow me is worthy of me. Those who gain their life will lose it, and those who lose their life for my sake will gain it. (Goodspeed)

Into a world controlled by sin was launched the life of Christ. The more completely he embodied the divine character and will, the more certain and intense would be the conflict between him and the powers dominating the old order. Any faith that takes the kingdom of God seriously has its fight cut out for it. Unless we accept our share of it, we are playing with our discipleship. But when the fight is for the kingdom of God, those who dodge, lose; and those who lose, win.

Our hearts burn within us as we follow the bleeding feet of thy Christ down the centuries, and count the mounts of anguish on which he was crucified anew in his prophets and the true apostles of his spirit. Help us to forgive those who did it, for some truly thought they were serving thee when they suppressed thy light, but, oh, save us from the same mistake!

Only Love Disarms

MATTHEW 5:44-45

God makes his sun to rise upon sinners as well as saints,
and sends rain upon the unjust and the just.

When we call out the militant spirit in religion, we summon a dangerous power. It has bred grimness and cruelty. Crusaders and inquisitors did their work in the name of Jesus, but not in his spirit. We must saturate ourselves with the spirit of our Master if our fighting is to further his kingdom. Hate breeds hate; force challenges force. Only love disarms; only forgiveness kills an enemy and leaves a friend. Jesus blended gentleness and virility, forgiving love and uncompromising boldness. He offered it as a mark of his kingdom that his followers used no force to defend him. Wherever they have done so, the kingdom of heaven has dropped to the level of the brutal empires. His attack is by the truth; whoever is won by that is conquered for good. Force merely changes the form of evil. When we "overcome evil with good," we eliminate it.

Suffer us not to turn in anger on one who has wronged us, lest we increase the sorrows of the world and taint our own souls with the poisoned sweetness of revenge.

The Great Initiator
of the Kingdom of God

MATTHEW 11:25-30

*Take my yoke upon you and learn of me, for I am gentle and
humble in heart, and you will find rest for your souls.*

Jesus had the consciousness of a unique relation to the
Father, which made him the mediator of a new understanding of God and of life. This new insight was making a new
intellectual alignment, leaving the philosophers and scholars as they were, and fertilizing the minds of simple people.
It is an historical fact that the brilliant body of intellectuals
of the first and second centuries was blind to what proved
to be the most fruitful and influential movement of all times,
and it was left to slaves and working people to transmit it
and save it from suppression at the cost of their lives.

Then Jesus turns to the toiling and heavy-laden people
about him with the offer of a new kind of leadership—none
of the brutal self-assertion of the Caesars and of all con-
querors here, but a gentle and humble spirit, and an obedience which was pleasure and brought release to the soul.

*Make us eager to pay the due price for what we get by
putting forth our own life in wholesome good will and
by bearing cheerily the troubles that go with all joys.*

The Most Poignant Consciousness of Sin

1 TIMOTHY 1:12-17

Faithful is the saying, and worthy of all acceptation,
that "Jesus Christ came into the world to save sinners"!
And there is no greater sinner than I! Yet for this very cause
I obtained mercy, so that in me, the chief of sinners,
Jesus Christ might display all his boundless patience.

We feel a deep consciousness of sin when we realize that we have wasted our years, dissipated our energies, left our opportunities unused, frustrated the grace of God, and dwarfed and shamed the personality which God intended when God called us into life. It is a similar and even deeper misery to realize that our past life has hurt or blocked the kingdom of God, the sum of all good, the essential aim of God. Our duty to the kingdom of God is on a higher level than all other duties. To aid it is the supreme joy. To have failed it by our weakness, to have hampered it by our ignorance, to have resisted its prophets, to have contradicted its truths, to have denied it in time of danger, to have betrayed it for thirty pieces of silver—this is the most poignant consciousness of sin.

If we have been engrossed in narrow duties and little questions, when the vast needs of humanity called aloud for prophetic vision and apostolic sympathy, we pray thee to forgive us.

The Purpose of the Church

1 PETER 2:1-10

You are the chosen race, the royal priesthood,
the consecrated nation, God's own people, so that
you may declare the virtues of him who called you out
of darkness into his wonderful light. (Goodspeed)

Since the kingdom of God is the supreme end of God, it must be the purpose for which the Church exists. The measure in which it fulfills this purpose is also the measure of its spiritual authority and honor. The institutions of the Church, its activities, its worship, and its theology must in the long run be tested by its effectiveness in creating the kingdom of God . . . The Church has the power to save insofar as the kingdom of God is present in it. If the Church is not living for the kingdom, its institutions are part of the "world." In that case it is not the power of redemption but its object. It may even become an anti-Christian power. If any form of church organization which formerly aided the kingdom now impedes it, the reason for its existence is gone.

Fit us for our work, lest we fail thee. We submit our
inmost desires to thy holy will, and beseech thee to make
thy law sweet to our willing hearts. Give, Lord, what thou
askest, and then ask what thou wilt. We make our prayer,
O God, by faith in Christ our Lord.

Maddening and Disarming Quietness

MARK 14:53-65

But Jesus remained silent, and answered nothing.

In the Sanhedrin, in the court of Pilate, amid the jests of the soldiers, Jesus had to live out the Father's mind and spirit. He did it in the combination of steadfastness and patience. The most striking thing in his bearing is his silence. He never yielded an inch, but neither did he strike back, or allow others to do it for him . . . He did not answer force by force, nor anger by anger. If he had, the world at that point would have subdued him and he would have fallen away from God. If he had headed the Galileans to storm Pilate's castle, he would have been a God-forsaken Christ.

But his attitude was not soft. He resisted. He fought. Even on the cross he fought. He never fought back so hard as then. But not with fist or stick on a physical level of brute force, but by the quietness which both maddens and disarms. If he had blustered, he would have been conquered. Christian art has misrepresented him when it makes him suffer with head down. His head was up and he was in command of the situation.

We praise thee for Jesus Christ, whose life has revealed to us your sacrificial love and the eternal law of the cross, and we rejoice that he has become the first-born among many brethren and sisters.

The Great Intensifier of Life

ROMANS 5:6-11

*God gives proof of his love to us by the fact that
while we were still sinners, Christ died for us.*

Selfishness always looks safe; love always looks like an enormous risk. We never live so intensely as when we love strongly. We never realize ourselves so vividly as when we are in the full glow of love for others. Love demands sacrifice, and sacrifice seems the denial and surrender of life. Actually, love is the great intensifier of life and giving our life preserves it. By seeking life selfishly, we lose it; when we lose it for love we gain it. We are far more active and self-assertive when we impart than when we receive. It is literally true that "it is more blessed to give than to receive." When people have lived for forty years and their desires begin to flag, the great test of age arrives. If they have identified themselves for years with some cause of humanity, working for it and suffering for it, their lives will have a meaning and a hope and a great pride to the end. But if they have fed no life but their own, they are locked in a gray prison which they have built for themselves. Such lives are truly old, even if their bodies are kept young by all the skill that money buys.

We praise thee for our brothers and sisters, artists and musicians, the masters of form and color and sound, who have power to unlock for us the vaster spaces of emotion and to lead us by their hand into the reaches of nobler passions. We rejoice in their gifts and pray thee to save them from the temptations which beset their powers. Save them from the discouragements of selfish ambition and from the vanity that feeds on cheap applause, from the snare of the senses and from the dark phantoms that haunt the listening soul.

The Thing We Live By

GALATIANS 5:13-15

For the whole Law has been fulfilled in this one precept,
Thou shalt love thy neighbor as thyself.

Jesus said that love is the supreme law of life and the thing we live by. Love validates the assertion. It pays as it goes. Nothing else does pay in the long run. The more true happiness and abiding satisfaction we have had from love, the more ought we to trust it as the true way of life. We must not only accept love and enjoy it when it comes to us, but we must seek it, cultivate it, and propagate it. It is not an incidental blessing, but the first and fundamental law of God, written in our hearts, and written large in all the world about us. When we heal love that has been torn, remove all contradictions of love from the outward relations of our life, and allow love to become our second nature, we shall deserve the highest patent of nobility—to be called daughters and sons of God. If love involves loss, we must accept the loss. Christ did. If selfishness seems to work better than love, we must have faith in love. Why else do we call ourselves Christians?

We pray thee to make the love of all true lovers strong, holy, and deathless, that no misunderstandings may fray the bond, and no gray disenchantment of the years may have power to quench the heavenly light that now glows in them. May they early gain wisdom to discern the true values of life, and may no tyranny of fashion and no glamor of cheaper joys filch from them the wholesome peace and inward satisfaction which only loyal love can give.

The Power of a Vital Faith

MATTHEW 14:22-33

*Then Peter got down from the boat and walked on the water to go
to Jesus. But when he saw the wind, he was afraid, and
as he began to sink, he cried out, "Master, save me!" At once
Jesus stretched out his hand and caught hold of him, saying
to him, "O little faith! What made you doubt?"*

A great task demands a great faith. To live a great life one
needs a great cause to which one can surrender, something
divinely large and engrossing for which one can live and if
need be, die. A great religious faith will lift one out of narrow grooves and be made an inspired instrument of the universal will of God. It is the point at which the human mind
coincides with the Eternal mind. A vital faith will gradually
saturate a person's whole life.

The force of will, of courage, of self-sacrifice liberated by
a living religious faith is so incalculable, so invincible, that
nothing is impossible when that power enters the field. The
author of the greatest revolution in history made the proposition that even the slightest amount of faith is competent
to do the unbelievable; faith as tiny as a mustard seed can
blast away mountains.

*Reveal to us the larger goodness and love that speak
through the unbending laws of thy world.*

Original Discipleship

LUKE 9:57-62

Go and announce, far and wide, the kingdom of God.

No one is a Christian in the full sense of the original discipleship until he or she has made the kingdom of God the controlling purpose of his or her life, and no one is intellectually prepared to understand Jesus Christ until he or she has understood the meaning of the kingdom of God. The Reformation of the sixteenth century was a revival of Pauline theology. The present-day Reformation is a revival of the spirit and aims of Jesus himself.

Grant us, we pray, the divine humility to realize that we are sent of thee as brothers and sisters and helpers of others and that the powers within us are but part of the vast equipment of humanity, entrusted to us for the common use. May we bow to the law of Christ and live, not to be served, but to give our abilities for the emancipation of the higher life of humanity. Save us from turning thy revelations into means of extortion.

An Intoxicating Power

LUKE 6:20-26

Blessed are you poor, for the kingdom of God is yours.
Blessed are you who are hungry now, for you shall be filled.
But woe to you rich! For you already have received your
consolation. Woe unto you who are full now!
For you shall suffer hunger.

The immense power wielded by the rich is an intoxicant that few can withstand permanently. People defer to them, smooth their way for them, and make them the center of every occasion. The morbid curiosity of the masses about their doings is unpleasant, but it is an expression of the sense of their importance. They acquire the seigniorial habit of mind and expect all things, including the law, to make room for them . . . Christianity gave a new valuation to the quality of humility in ethics. Humility is the sense of dependence on others, the feeling that whatever we have has been received from God and our fellow human beings, and that we find our true life only as serviceable members of the social organism.

Behold the servants of Mammon, who nullify by their craft the merciful laws which nobler ones have devised for the protection of the weak.

Forming Christian Revolutionists

MARK 8:31-38

Your thoughts are not God's thoughts, but human thoughts.

The individual and collective life of humanity act and react on each other. Every changed individual life makes a changed society possible. Every change for the better in the institutions of society makes a higher perfection of the individual possible. Each is an originating center of power. Each, therefore, is a citadel to be captured in the name of God.

The Christian Church must enlist the will and love of men and women for God, mark them with the cross of Christ, and send them out to finish up the work which Christ began. Is the Church supplying society with the necessary equipment of such personalities? Let us grant that it can never reach all; but is it making Christian revolutionists of those whom it does teach and control?

O God, we pray thee for those who come after us. We are wasting the resources of the earth in our headlong greed, and they will suffer want. We are building sunless houses and joyless cities for our profit, and they must dwell therein. We are making the burden heavy and the pace of work pitiless, and they will fall wan and sobbing by the wayside. We are poisoning the air of our land by our lies and our uncleanness, and they will breathe it. Grant us grace to leave the earth fairer than we found it.

The Church's Orientation

LUKE 12:22-32

Be not anxious about your life. But seek God's kingdom.
Fear not, little flock, for it is your Father's good pleasure
to give you the kingdom.

We do not substitute social activities for religion . . . If the Church comes to lean on social preachings and doings as a crutch because its religion has become paralytic, may the Lord have mercy on us all! We do not want less religion; we want more; but it must be a religion that gets its orientation from the kingdom of God. To concentrate our efforts on personal salvation, or on soul culture, comes close to refined selfishness. All who have been trained in egotistic religion need a conversion to Christian Christianity. Seek first the kingdom of God and God's righteousness, and the salvation of your soul will be added to you.

Help us to make our city the mighty common workshop of our people, where every one will find a place and task. Bind our citizens, not by the bond of money and of profit alone, but by the glow of neighborly good-will, by the thrill of common joys, and the pride of common possessions. If in the past there have been some who have sold the city's good for private gain, staining her honor by their cunning and greed, fill us, we beseech thee, with the righteous anger of true sons and daughters that we may purge out the shame lest it taint the future years.

For the Present We Are Here

LUKE 10:1-11

But know this, that the kingdom of God
is drawing near to you.

This earth is even now the habitation of God, and it is ours to make it wholly so. It is not a place to be spurned, but a home to be loved and made clean and holy . . . This joyful religious acceptance of the present life involves no surrender of the life to come. When our work for God is done and we are tired, when our growth in God has exhausted the opportunities offered by the present life, we can lie down secure in the hope that our life will unfold in greater fullness in a new environment adapted to the garnered results of the present life. But for the present we are here. Here we must see our visions, and here we must realize them. The hope of the kingdom of God makes this earth the theater of action, and turns the full force of religious will and daring toward the present tasks.

If soon we must go, yet through thee we have lived and our life flows on in humanity. By thy grace we too have helped to shape the future and bring in the better day.

When Christianity Is a Terrible Thing

JOHN 21:15-19

Do you love me?

Remember that loving means loving. It doesn't mean smiling and complimenting our neighbors to their faces and running pins in their reputations behind their backs . . . Loving means loving . . . This Christianity is a terrible thing when you get it undiluted from the very source. Jesus tells us to love our neighbors and love them as well as ourselves. Nothing remains for us to do but to settle down and do as well as we can.

We thank thee for the revealing power of love which divines in the one beloved the mystic beauty and glory of humanity. We thank thee for the transfiguring power of love which ripens and ennobles our nature, calling forth the hidden stores of tenderness and strength and overcoming the selfishness of youth by the passion of self-surrender.

The Living Germ
of the Kingdom

MATTHEW 5:13-16

You are the salt of the earth. You are the light of the world.

Christ initiated his kingdom on earth by establishing a community of spiritual individuals, in inward communion with God and in outward obedience to God. This was the living germ of the kingdom. But it was not the purpose of this community merely to dismiss one after another of its members into heaven and leave the world as it was, nor was the increase of its membership the only method of extending its power. By the power of the Spirit dwelling in it, it was to overcome the spirit dominant in the world and thus penetrate and transform the world. Within this community Christ reigns, here his laws prevail, and his Spirit is the governing force. If Christ's purpose had been merely the conversion of individuals, the formation of the Church would have been useful but not essential. Because his purpose was the immediate establishment and extension of a kingdom, a society was absolutely essential.

Save us from the deadly poison of class-pride. Grant that we may look everyone in the face with the eyes of love. If any one needs us, make us ready to yield our help ungrudgingly, unless higher duties claim us, and may we rejoice that we have it in us to be helpful to our fellows.

The Sacredness of Life

MATTHEW 8:1-4

Jesus stretched out his hand and touched him.
"I do choose," he said, "become clean."

Whenever Jesus healed he rendered a social service to his fellows. The spontaneous tenderness which he put into his contact with the sick was an expression of his sense of the sacredness of life. A leper with fingerless hands and decaying joints was repulsive to the aesthetic feelings and a menace to selfish fear of infection. The community quarantined the lepers in waste places by stoning them when they crossed bounds. Jesus not only healed this man, but his sense of humanity so went out to him that he stretched forth his hand and touched him. Even the most wretched specimen of humanity still had value to Jesus.

We might have followed thy blessed footsteps, O Christ, binding up the bruised hearts of our brothers and sisters. Instead there are poor hearts now broken and darkened because they encountered us on the way, and some perhaps remember us only as the beginning of their misery or sin.

Beyond Theology
and the Bible

LUKE 8:5-15

*The seed in the good soil is those who have listened
to the message and, in an honest and good heart,
hold it fast, and bring forth fruit with patience.*

People are so afraid of religious vagaries, and so little afraid of religious stagnation. Yet the religion of Jesus has less to fear from sitting down to meat with publicans and sinners than from the immaculate isolation of the pious. It will take care of itself if mixed into three measures of meal; but if the leaven is kept standing by itself it will sour hopelessly. If the Church tries to confine itself to theology and the Bible, and refuses its larger mission to humanity, its theology will gradually become mythology and its Bible a closed book. If the gospel lags behind and deals in outgrown conceptions of life and duty, it will lose power over the ablest minds and the young first, and gradually over all. The Church cannot afford to have the young sniff the air as in a stuffy room when they enter the sphere of religious thought.

Grant that in us the faith in thy parenthood may shine through all our life with such persuasive beauty that some who still creep in the dusk of fear may stand erect as free children of God, and that those who now through unbelief are living as orphans in an empty world may stretch out their hands to the great Lover of their spirits and find thee near.

Not about the Church

EPHESIANS 2:11-22

*Take notice then that no longer are you strangers
and foreigners, but you are fellow citizens with the saints and
members of God's household. You are built upon the foundation
of the apostles and prophets, Jesus Christ himself being
the chief cornerstone. In him you are continuously built
together for a dwelling-place of God through his Spirit.*

Religion is not a purely individual matter. Nothing in human life is. We are social beings, and all elements of our life come to their full development only through social interchange and co-operation. Our pleasures, our affections, our moral aspirations are all lifted to higher power and scope by sharing them with others. It stands to reason that religion, too, demands social expression and will come to its full strength and richness only when it is shared with others. The Christian Church is not an end in itself. It is always a means to an end. It is to create and foster the religious life in the individual; it is to build up the kingdom of God in all humanity.

The historical Christ, the invisible Spirit, the visible Church—these are the forces of God in human history. And they are revolutionary forces.

As we have thirsted with evil passions to the destruction of people, do thou fill us now with hunger and thirst for justice that we may bear glad tidings to the poor and set at liberty all who are in the prison-house of want and sin.

Make a Place for God

1 JOHN 4:7-21

*God is love, and those who abide in love abide in God,
and God abides in them.*

We assume that love to God must come first and is the proper starting point and foundation for the love of others. Is it not just as much the other way? The love of others is our concrete object lesson in the kindergarten of love, and if we learn that well, and as fast as we learn that well, the love of God grows in us, and we become religious . . . In other words, God is invisible and inaccessible, but if we love one another, we make a place for God in our own life and will realize God and God's love.

Our Father, thou art the final source of all our comforts and to thee we render thanks for our food. But we also remember in gratitude the many men and women whose labor was necessary to produce it, and who gathered it from the land and afar from the sea for our sustenance. Grant that they too may enjoy the fruit of their labor without want and may be bound up with us in a fellowship of thankful hearts.

Unto Me

MATTHEW 25:40

You have done it unto me.

When Jesus looked forward to the great climax of History, the Last Judgment, he saw it as a process by which the inner significance of their own actions and relations would be revealed to men and women. Those on his right hand whom he welcomed to their reward had never realized the high quality of their own actions . . . They all thought they had done [actions of service] for folks—for dirty, sweaty, tired, discouraged individuals. But Jesus says: "Oh, no, ye did it unto me. My life is so identified with my brothers and sisters that when ye fed and clothed them, ye fed and clothed me. God is living in these worn human bodies. When ye comforted them, ye comforted God."

O Jesus, we thy servants bow before thee to confess the common sins of our calling. Thou knowest all things; thou knowest that we love thee and that our hearts' desire is to serve thee in faithfulness; and, yet, like Peter, we have so often failed thee in the hour of thy need.

In the Footsteps of Jesus

LUKE 19:1-10

For the Son of man has come to seek and to save the lost.

Social workers are in the direct line of apostolic succession. Like the Son of Man they seek and save the lost. Their work is redemptive work . . . They are treading step by step in the footprints of Jesus of Nazareth, and they have a right to feel the nearness and love of their Heavenly Father in doing it, just as Jesus felt it. They are doing Christlike work when they do social work, even if they themselves disclaim religious motives or even repudiate religious faith. Jesus found society nicely separated into pious people on the one side and publicans and sinners on the other, but he found the classification not in harmony with the facts. The publicans and sinners were showing all the symptoms of religion and the pious people turned their backs on God whenever they had a chance.

We praise thee, O God, for our friends and fellow workers, for the touch of their hands and the brightness of their faces, for the cheer of their words and the outflow of good will that refreshes us. Grant us the insight of love that we may see them as thou seest, not as frail mortals, but as radiant children of God who have wrought patience out of tribulation and who bear in earthen vessels the treasures of thy grace.

No Love, No Christian

1 JOHN 3:10-11

No one who does not act uprightly or who does not love their brother or sister is a child of God. For the message you have heard from the beginning is this: We must love one another.

(Goodspeed)

These words were meant to repudiate the claim to Christian standing of anyone whose religion was not grounded deep in active and passionate good will toward others. Moreover, in Christianity love must mean more than mild benevolence of feeling. Love gets its Christian definition from the personality of Jesus and from his death. The insistence that love to God must have its immediate result and counterpoise in love of others is one of the rudiments of Christian faith and feeling.

May thy Spirit, O God, which is ceaselessly pleading within us, prevail at last to bring our business life under Christ's law of service, so that all who share in the processes of factory and trade may grow up into that high consciousness of a divine calling which blesses those who are the free servants of God and the people who consciously devote their strength to the common good.

Working Sacramental Miracles

ROMANS 11:33-36

For of God and through God and for God are all things.
All glory to God forever and ever!

The kingdom of God deals not only with the immortal soul of mortals, but with their bodies, their nourishment, their homes, their cleanliness, and it makes those who serve these fundamental needs of life veritable ministers of God. Are they not serving the common good? Are they not working sacramental miracles by cooperating with that mysterious power which satisfies the want of every living thing by making the grain and the tree to grow? If they do their job well, that job itself is their chief ministry to others and part of their worship of God. Whenever they strive to increase their serviceableness to humanity, they make another advance toward the kingdom of God.

We praise thee, O God, for our friends, the doctors and
nurses, who seek the healing of our bodies. We bless thee
for their gentleness and patience, for their knowledge and
skill. Make thou our doctors the prophets and soldiers
of thy kingdom, which is the reign of cleanliness and
self-restraint and the dominion of health and joyous life.
Strengthen in their whole profession the consciousness
that their calling is holy and that they, too, are disciples
of the saving Christ.

The True Revolutionists and Pilgrims of This World

ROMANS 8:6-17, 26-27

*Only those are children of God who are led by God's Spirit,
and if children of God, then heirs, heirs of God
and joint-heirs with Christ Jesus.*

It seems to me that to possess the Spirit of God is the most effective revolutionary equipment. Those that have it are independent above anyone in the world. They have the great Companion ever with them, whose presence Jesus declared to be better than his own visible companionship. They can at any time lean back and feel the Eternal Rock supporting them. They stand among their neighbors in state and church, sharing with them, serving them, but not mastered by them. The feeble aspirations of their fluttering human spirit are borne up on the eagle wings of that mightier Spirit. Their conscience is quickened and steadied by reference to that inward guide . . . The true revolutionists, the pilgrims of this world, the children of eternity need that abiding Presence if they would have wisdom not to stumble at the critical movement, boldness not to flinch, strength to seize the opportunity, and a serene and hopeful faith that even a desert wind cannot scorch.

Help us to make our community the greater home of our people, where all may live their lives in comfort, unafraid, living their lives in peace and rounding out their years in strength. May we remember that our community's true wealth and greatness consist not in the abundance of the things we possess, but in the justice of her institutions and the kinship of her children. Make her rich in her sons and daughters and famous through the lofty passions that inspire them.

Love and Justice

1 CORINTHIANS 1:26-31

You are God's children, through your union with Christ Jesus, whom God has made our wisdom—our uprightness and consecration and redemption. (Goodspeed)

Mark well: Christ's commandment of love presupposes the world's commandment of justice. Justice is the foundation on which love can build its temple. Unless that foundation is there, the walls will crack.

It is necessary to say this because so many try to be loving without being just. Workers are fond of saying, "We want justice, not charity." It is a good saying. Perhaps it would be better to say, "First justice, then charity." After justice has been done, there will still be ample room for love, and then it will be love indeed and not "charity."

We pray thee for the lords of industry and trade in whose hands the wealth and power of our modern world have gathered. We beseech thee to save them from the terrible temptations of their position, lest they follow in the somber lineage of those who have lorded it in the past and have used the people's powers for their oppression.

Being Made New

COLOSSIANS 2:8-15

*In baptism you were raised with him, through your faith
in the energy of that God who raised him from the dead.
And you also God has made alive together with Christ.*

The fundamental contribution of every person is the change of one's own personality. We must repent of the sins of existing society, cast off the spell of the lies protecting our social wrongs, have faith in a higher social order, and realize in ourselves a new type of Christian personhood which seeks to overcome the evil in the present world, not by withdrawing from the world, but by revolutionizing it.

*For every harm we have done, may we do some brave act
of salvation, and that for every soul that has stumbled or
fallen through us, may we bring to thee some other weak
or despairing one, whose strength has been renewed by
our love, that so the face of thy Christ may smile upon us
and the light within us may shine undimmed.*

The Greatest of These

1 CORINTHIANS 12:31

I will go on to show you a still more excellent way.

If I create wealth beyond the dreams of past ages and increase not love, my heat is the flush of fever and my success will deal death.

Though I have foresight to locate the foundations of riches, and power to preempt them, and skill to tap them, and have no loving vision for humanity, I am blind.

Though I give my profits to the poor and make princely endowments for those who toil for me, if I have no human fellowship of life with them, my life is barren and doomed.

Love is just and kind. Love is not greedy and covetous. Love exploits no one; it takes no unearned gain; it gives more than it gets. Love does not break down the lives of others to make wealth for itself; it makes wealth to build the life of all. Love seeks solidarity; it tolerates no divisions; it prefers equal workmates; it shares its efficiency. Love enriches all people, educates all people, gladdens all people.

The values created by love never fail; but whether there are class privileges, they shall fail; whether there are millions gathered, they shall be scattered; and whether there are vested rights, they shall be abolished. For in the past the strong lorded it in ruthlessness and strove for their own power and pride, but when the perfect social order comes, the strong shall serve the common good. Before the sun of Christ brought in the dawn, people competed, and forced tribute from weakness, but when the full day shall come, they will work as mates in love, each for all and all for each.

For now we see in the fog of selfishness, darkly, but then with social vision; now we see our fragmentary ends but then we shall see the destinies of all as God sees them. But now abideth honor, justice, and love, these three; and the greatest of these is love.

Accept the work of this day, O Lord, as we lay it at thy feet.

We Need Each Other

EPHESIANS 4:1-6

*I summon you to live lives worthy of the calling to which you
were called. With all humility and gentleness and long-suffering
forbear with one another in love; and endeavor to preserve
the unity of the Spirit in the bonds of peace.*

The kingdom of God is what Jesus came and died for. The
kingdom of God, my friend, is a social conception. It is
a conception for this life here of ours, because Jesus says,
"Thy kingdom come. Thy will be done" here. It is something that is here on this earth; that quietly pervades all
humanity; that is always working toward the perfect life
of God. It cannot be lived out by you alone—you have
got to live it out with me, and with that brother or sister sitting before you. We, together, have to work it out. It
is a matter of community life. The perfect community of
human beings—that would be the kingdom of God! With
God above them; with their brother or sister next to them—
clasping hands in kinship, doing the work of justice—that is
the kingdom of God.

*Suffer us not to grieve those whom thou hast sent to us as
the sweet ministers of love. May our eyes not be so holden
by selfishness that we know thine angels only when they
spread their wings to return to thee.*

The Common Journey

Stand for the Solidarity of Humanity

Our personality is of divine and eternal value,
but we see it aright
only when we see it as part of humankind.
Our religious individuality
must get its interpretation from the supreme fact
of social solidarity.
Prayer ought to be a keen realization of our fellows,
and not a forgetfulness of the world.

Walter Rauschenbusch
"Christianizing the Social Order"
1912

*Now unto him who, according to his might that is at
work within us, is able to do infinitely more than all we
ask or even think, to him be the glory in the church and
in Christ Jesus, to all generations, world without end.
Amen.* (Ephesians 3:20-21)

Solidarity of Humanity

ACTS 17:22-28

*The God who made the universe and all things in it gives
to all life and breath and all things. God has made of one
blood every nation to dwell on all the face of the earth.
In God we live and move and have our being.*

Christianity stands for the doctrine that we must love one another—everyone, without distinction . . . It does not call on the strong to climb in isolation across the backs of the weak, but challenges them to prove their strength by lifting the rest with them . . . It stands for the solidarity of humanity in its weakness and strength, its defeat and conquests, its sin and salvation.

May we, who now live, see the oncoming of the great day of God, when all people shall stand side by side in equal worth and real freedom, all toiling and all reaping, masters of nature but brothers and sisters with one another, exultant in the tide of the common life, and jubilant in the adoration of thee, the source of their blessings and Father of us all.

An Affirmation of Faith

ISAIAH 46:8-11

Remember this and consider, recall it to mind; I am God, and there is no one like me. I have spoken, and I will bring it to pass. I have planned, and I will do it. (NRSV)

I affirm my faith in the reality of the spiritual world, in the sacred voice of duty, in the compelling power of truth and holiness, in prayer, in the life eternal, in the One who is the life of my life and the reality behind all things visible. I rejoice to believe in God.

I affirm my faith in the kingdom of God and my hope in its final triumph. I determine by faith to live day by day within the higher order and divine peace of my true father-hood, and to carry its spirit and laws into all my dealings in the world that now is.

I make an act of love toward all fellow human beings. I accept them as they are, with all their sins and failures, and declare my solidarity with them. If any have wronged or grieved me, I place my mind within the all-comprehending and all-loving mind of God, and here and now forgive. I desire to minister God's love to all people, and to offer no hindrance to the free flow of God's love through me.

I affirm my faith in life. I call life good and not evil. I accept the limitations of my own life and believe that it is possible for me to live a beautiful and Christlike life within the conditions set for me. Through the power of Christ which descends on me, I know that I can be more than conqueror. Amen.

Enlarge within us the sense of fellowship with all the living things to whom thou hast given this earth as their home in common with us.

Jesus of the Common People

LUKE 19:28-48

*And when now he was coming near Jerusalem, and
descending the Mount of Olives, the whole multitude
of the disciples began to rejoice, and to praise God with
a loud voice for all the mighty works they had seen.*

Jesus proceeded from the common people . . . The common people heard him gladly because he said what was in their hearts. His triumphal entry into Jerusalem was a poor man's procession; the coats from their backs were his tapestry; their throats his brass band, and a donkey was his steed. During the last days in Jerusalem he was constantly walking into the lion's cage and brushing the sleeve of death. It was the fear of the people which protected him while he bearded the powers that be. His midnight arrest, his hasty trial, the anxious efforts to work on the feelings of the crowd against him, were all a tribute to his standing with the common people.

By birth and training, by moral insight and conviction, by his sympathy for those who were down, and by his success in winning them to his side, Jesus was a man of the common people, and he never deserted their cause as so many others have done. Whenever the people have caught a glimpse of him as he really was, their hearts have hailed Jesus of Nazareth as one of them.

*Give thy church faith to espouse the cause of the people,
and in their hands that grope after freedom and light to
recognize the bleeding hands of the Christ.*

The Only True Life

JOHN 10:1-10

I have come that they may have life,
and may have it in abundance.

Jesus was not a child of this world. He did not revere those it called great; he did not accept its customs and social usages as final; his moral conceptions did not run along the grooves marked out by it. He nourished within his soul the ideal of a common life so radically different from the present that it involved a reversal of values, a revolutionary displacement of existing relations. This ideal was not merely a beautiful dream to solace his soul. He lived it out in his own daily life. He urged others to live that way. He held that it was the only true life, and that the ordinary way was misery and folly. He dared to believe that it would triumph. When he saw that the people were turning from him and that his nation had chosen the evil way and was drifting toward the rocks that would destroy it, unutterable sadness filled his soul, but he never abandoned his faith in the final triumph of that kingdom of God for which he had lived. For the present, the cross; but beyond the cross, the kingdom of God. If he was not to achieve it now, he would return and do it then.

For all the oppressed afar off who sigh for liberty; for all lovers of the people who strive to break their shackles; for all who dare to believe in democracy and the kingdom of God, make thou our great commonwealth once more a sure beacon-light of hope and a guide on the path which leads to the perfect union of law and liberty.

Splinter the Old to Make Way for the New

ACTS 17:1-9

*These people who have upset the habitable earth are
come hither also. They all act contrary of the decrees
of Caesar, saying there is another king, one Jesus.*

The spirit of primitive Christianity did not spread only sweet
peace and tender charity, but the leaven of social unrest. It
caused some to thrown down their tools and quit work. It
stirred women to break down the restraints of custom and
modesty. It invaded the intimacies of domestic relations and
threatened families with disruption. It awakened slaves to
a sense of worth and a longing for freedom which made
slavery doubly irksome and strained their relations to their
masters. It disturbed the patriotism and loyalty of citizens
for the country and intervened between the sovereign state
and its subjects.

All this is neither strange nor reprehensible. No great historic revolution has ever worked its way without breaking
and splintering the old to make way for the new. New wine
is sure to ferment and burst the old wineskins. Moreover,
it is likely to taste sour and yeasty, and some will say, "The
old is better."

Our argument here is simply this, that Christianity must
have had a strong social impetus to evoke such stirrings of
social unrest and discontent. It was not purely religious,
but also a democratic and social movement. Or, to state it
far more truly: it was so strongly and truly religious that it
was of necessity democratic and social. Thus Christianity

as a social movement was launched with all the purpose
and hope, all the impetus and power, of a great revolutionary movement pledged to change the world-as-it-is into the
world-as-it-ought-to-be.

*We bless thee for the inspired souls of all ages who saw
afar the shining city of God, and by faith left the profit of
the present to follow their vision.*

The Land

PSALM 24

*The earth is the L*ORD*'s and all that is in it, the world,*
and those who live in it. (NRSV)

Next to life itself, the greatest gift of God to mortals is the land from which all life is nourished. The character of a nation cannot be understood apart from the country and climate in which it lives. The social prosperity, the morality, the rise or decline of a people, always fundamentally depend on the wisdom and justice with which the land is distributed and used. In our country the land in its vastness and abundance, its variety and wealth, has been one of the most sanitary influences in our national life. Nearly all ancient communities with which we have historic connection recognized that the community is the real owner of the land. But now that our free lands are almost exhausted, we have come to the point where elements of injustice in the system will begin to menace us. Those who have the soil have that and their bodies to work it. Those who have no soil have only their bodies, and they must work for the others to get bread. They are the disinherited children of our nation. What God gave for the support of all will be the special privilege of some.

The moral problem to be solved by us is how to safeguard the rights of the individual holder of the land who has increased its value by labor and intelligence, and yet to extract for the community the value which the community creates.

When our use of this world is over and we make room for others, may we not leave anything ravished by our greed or spoiled by our ignorance, but may we hand on our common heritage fairer and sweeter through our use of it, undiminished in fertility and joy, that so our bodies may return in peace to the great mother who nourished them and our spirits may round the circle of a perfect life in thee.

The Incarnational Church

1 JOHN 2:3-6

Those who say, "I remain in him" ought to spend
their lives as he spent his.

If the Church is to have saving power, it must embody Christ. He is the revolutionary force within it. The saving qualities of the Church depend on the question whether it has translated the personal life of Jesus Christ into the social life of its group and thus bring it to bear on the individual. The Church is to be the incarnation of the Christ-spirit on earth, the organized conscience of Christendom. It should be swiftest to awaken to every undeserved suffering, bravest to speak against every wrong, and strongest to rally the moral forces of the community against everything that threatens the better life among people. The Church furnishes Christ with lips to speak his thoughts, with feet to go his errands, with hands to lift up the sick and to check the blow of cruelty. Generally speaking, if the Church is paralyzed and irresponsive to the will of the Head, or if it has fallen to reveling and made itself drunk with the wine of Mammon, then the will of Christ will remain unperformed.

Put upon thy Church a more imperious responsiveness
to duty, a swifter compassion with suffering, and an utter
loyalty to the will of God.

The Magic and Mythology of War

JAMES 3:13-18

*The fruit of righteousness is being sown in peace
by those who are working peace.*

Wherever militarism rules, war is idealized by monuments and paintings, poetry and song. The stench of hospitals and the maggots of the battlefield are passed in silence, and the imagination of the people is filled with waving plumes and the shout of charging columns. If war is ever to be relegated to the limbo of outgrown barbarism, we must shake off its magic. When we comprehend how few wars ever have been fought for the sake of justice or the people; how personal spite, the ambition of military professionals, and the protection of capitalistic ventures are the real moving powers; how the governing classes pour out the blood and wealth of nations for private ends and exude patriotic enthusiasm like a squid secreting ink to hide its retreat—then the mythology of war will no longer bring us to our knees, and we shall fail to get drunk with the rest when martial intoxication sweeps the people off their feet.

Ever the songs of the past and the pomp of armies have been used to inflame the passions of people. Our spirit cries out to thee in revolt against it, and we know that our righteous anger is answered by thy holy wrath. Break thou the spell of the enchantments that make the nations drunk with the lust of battle and draw them on as willing tools of death.

Lies Dressed Up in Truth

ISAIAH 28:14-17

*Because you have said, "We have made lies our refuge,
and in falsehood we have taken shelter"; therefore says
the LORD God, "I will make justice the line, and
righteousness the plummet; hail will sweep away the
refuge of lies, and waters will overwhelm the shelter." (NRSV)*

We shall have to see through the fictions of capitalism. We are assured that the poor are poor through their own fault; that rent and profits are the just dues of foresight and ability; that the immigrants are the cause of corruption in our city politics; that we cannot compete with foreign countries unless our working class will descend to the wages paid abroad. These are very plausible assertions, but they are lies dressed up in truth. There is a great deal of conscious lying. In the main these misleading theories are the complacent self-deception of those who profit by present conditions and are loath to believe that their life is working harm.

The greatest contribution which anyone can make to the social movement is the contribution of a regenerated personality, of a will which sets justice above policy and profit, and of an intellect emancipated from falsehood.

We plead with thee, O God, for those who are pressed by the cares and beset by the temptations of business life. As long as one person is set against another in a struggle for wealth, help those in business to make their contest, as far as may be, a test of excellence, by which the defeated may be spurred to better work. If anyone is pitted against those

138

who have forgotten fairness and honesty, help them to put their trust resolutely in the profitableness of sincerity and uprightness, and, if need be, to accept loss rather than follow on crooked paths.

All Life Filled with Divine Purpose

PSALM 8

*O LORD, our Sovereign, how majestic is your name
in all the earth!* (NRSV)

If now we could have faith enough to believe that all human life can be filled with divine purpose; that God saves not only the soul, but the whole of human life; that anything which serves to make people healthy, intelligent, happy, and good is a service to the Father of all; that the kingdom of God is not bounded by the Church, but includes all human relations—then all professions would be hallowed and receive religious dignity. Someone making shoes or arguing a law case or planting potatoes or teaching school could feel that this was itself a contribution to the welfare of humankind, and indeed one's main contribution to it.

Gladden us by the glowing consciousness of the one life that thinks and strives in us all, and knit us together into a commonwealth of brothers and sisters in which each shall be heir of all things and the free servant of all people.

The Manifest Will of God

MICAH 6:6-8

*He has told you, O mortal, what is good; and what does
the LORD require of you but to do justice, and to love kindness,
and to walk humbly with your God?* (NRSV)

The great aim underlying the whole social movement is the
creation of a free, just, and charitable social order. This is
the greatest moral task conceivable. Its accomplishment is
the manifest will of God for this generation. Every Christian motive is calling us to it. If it is left undone, millions of
lives will be condemned to a deepening moral degradation
and to spiritual starvation. Does it look probable that we
shall lose our contact with God if we plunge too deeply into
this work? Does it stand to reason that we shall go astray
from Jesus Christ if we engage in the unequal conflict with
organized wrong? What kind of "spirituality" is it which is
likely to get hurt by being put to work for justice and our
fellow human beings?

*Show thy erring children at last the way from the City of
Destruction to the City of Love, and fulfill the longings
of the prophets of humanity. Our Master, once more we
make thy faith our prayer: "Thy kingdom come! Thy will
be done on earth!"*

A Sacrament of Humanity

MATTHEW 10:40-42

Those who give to drink to one of these little ones
a cup of cold water only, I tell you in solemn truth,
shall not lose their reward.

We are all blind to the religious significance of our own lives. We are always in danger of doing high and holy things in a petty and worldly way. Jesus was always uncovering the spiritual meaning in the common actions of life. To Jesus giving a cup of cold water was a sacrament of humanity. Social workers are dealing with people, with folks, in a very human way. But they are also dealing with the Christ who is the champion and savior of the people, and with the eternal God in whom these people live and move and have their being.

Lay thy Spirit upon us and inspire us with a passion of Christlike love that we may join our lives to the weak and oppressed and may strengthen their cause by bearing their sorrows. Make us determined to love even at cost to our pride, that so we may be instruments of thy peace.

Submission

LUKE 1:26-38

Let it be to me as you have said.

We love and serve God when we love and serve our neighbors, whom God loves and in whom God lives. We rebel against God and repudiate God's will when we set our profit and ambition above the welfare of our neighbors and above the kingdom of God which binds them together. Sin is essentially selfishness. The sinful mind, then, is the unsocial and anti-social mind. In some germinal and rudimentary form salvation must turn us from a life centered on ourselves toward a life going out toward God and others. God is the all-embracing source and exponent of the common life and good of humankind. We must submit to God, we must submit to the supremacy of the common good. Salvation is the voluntary socializing of the soul.

O God, we worship thee as the sole lord and sovereign of humanity, and render free obedience to thee because thy laws are just and thy will is love.

God Made Us for One Another

HEBREWS 10:19-25

*Let us hold fast the confession of our hope, unwavering; and
let us consider one another, to provoke unto love and good works;
not forsaking the assembling of ourselves together.*

The mystic way to holiness is not through humanity but
above it. We can not set aside the fundamental law of God
that way. God made us for one another, and our highest
perfection comes not by isolation but by love. The way of
holiness through human fellowship and service is slower
and lowlier, but its results are more essentially Christian. . . .
[Paul's] great chapter on love is offered as a counter-poise
and antidote to the dangers of mysticism.

I believe in prayer and meditation in the presence of God;
in the conscious purging of the soul from fear, love of gain,
and selfish ambition, through realizing God; in bringing the
intellect into alignment with the mind of Christ; and in re-af-
firming the allegiance of the will to the kingdom of God.
Personal sanctification must serve the kingdom of God.

*Bless thou that great family of humanity of which we are
but a little part. Give to all thy children their daily bread,
and let our family not enjoy its comforts in selfish isolation.*

Anthropocentric Mysticism

MATTHEW 25:31-40

*In solemn truth I tell you that inasmuch as you
have done it unto one of the least of these,
you have done it unto me.*

The saint of the future will need not only a theocentric mysticism which enables one to realize God, but an anthropocentric mysticism which enables one to realize one's fellow human beings in God. The more we approach pure Christianity, the more will the Christian signify one who loves humankind with a religious passion and excludes none. The feeling which Jesus had when he said, "I am the hungry, the naked, the lonely," will be in the emotional consciousness of all holy ones in the coming days. The sense of solidarity is one of the distinctive marks of the true followers of Jesus.

Lift the veil of the future and show us the generation to come as it will be if blighted by our guilt, that our lust may be cooled and we may walk in the fear of the Eternal. Grant us a vision of the far-off years as they may be if redeemed by the sons and daughters of God, that we may take heart and do battle for thy children and ours.

What Our Nation Needs

EZEKIEL 18:30-32

Get yourselves a new heart and a new spirit!
Turn, then, and live. (NRSV)

Mending the social order is not like repairing a clock in which one or two parts are broken. It is rather like restoring diseased or wasted tissues, and when that has to be done, every organ and cell of the body is heavily taxed. During the reconstructive process every one of us must be an especially good cell in whatever organ of the social body we happen to be located. It is not this or that thing our nation needs, but a new mind and heart, a new conception of the way we all ought to live together, a new conviction about the worth of a human life and the use God wants us to make of our own lives. We want revolution both inside and outside.

O God, save us, for our nation is at strife with its own soul and is sinning against the light which thou aforetime hast kindled in it.

Love Demands Solidarity

MATTHEW 22:35-40

*"You must love the Lord your God with your whole heart, your
whole soul, and your whole mind." That is the great, first
command. There is a second like it: "You must love your
neighbor as you do yourself." (Goodspeed)*

Which among the multitudinous prescriptions of the Jewish
law ought to take precedence of the rest? It was a fine aca-
demic question for church lawyers to discuss. Jesus passed
by all ceremonial and ecclesiastical requirements, and put
his hand on love as the central law of life, both in religion
and ethics. It was a great simplification and spiritualization
of religion. But love is the social instinct which binds people together and makes them indispensable to one another.
Whoever demands love, demands solidarity. Whoever sets
love first, sets fellowship high.

*Thy Christ has kindled in us the passion for brotherhood
and sisterhood, but the social life we have built denies and
slays brotherhood and sisterhood.*

Solidarity and Forgiveness

MATTHEW 18:21-22

Master, how many times am I to forgive another who
wrongs me? Seven times over? "Not seven times over,
I tell you, but seventy-seven times over!" (Goodspeed)

Love binds together; hate and anger cut apart. They destroy fellowship. Therefore, the chief effort of the Christian spirit must be to reestablish fellowship wherever people have been sundered by ill-will. This is done by confession and forgiveness. Forgiveness was so important to Jesus because social unity was so important to him. In the Lord's Prayer he makes full fellowship with others a condition of full fellowship with God: "Forgive us our debts, as we forgive our debtors." Not to forgive is to put ourselves outside the pale of God's forgiveness, for our debt to God is to our neighbor's debt to us as twelve million dollars is to thirty-five dollars. If the other has no sense of wrong, it is still not right for us to leave the matter as it is. The initiative of reconciliation lies with us, and we are not excused till we have tried all means to convince the other of the wrong done. The desire to forgive must always be present. Christ prayed the Father to forgive those who crucified him, although they asked for no forgiveness. He forgave Peter though we know of no request for forgiveness but only of tears. Love survives wrong. And love overcomes wrong.

If we remember that any brother or sister justly hath
aught against us through this day's work, fix in us this
moment the firm resolve to make good the wrong and
to win again the love of our sister or brother.

The Final Test of All

MATTHEW 25:31-32, 41-46

*In solemn truth I tell you that inasmuch as you
did not do it unto one of these least,
you did not do it unto me.*

"Whence he shall come to judge the quick and the dead."
Think of it—absolute justice done at last, by an all-know-
ing Judge, where no earthly pull of birth, wealth, learning,
or power will count, and where all masks fall! By what code
of law and what standard shall we be judged there? Here is
the answer of Jesus: Not by creed and church questions, but
by our human relations; by the reality of our social feeling;
by our practical solidarity with our fellow human beings. If
we lived in the presence of hunger, loneliness, and oppression and remained apathetic, out we go. You and I—to the
right or the left?

*O God, thou great Redeemer of humankind, our hearts
are tender in the thought of thee, for in all the afflictions
of humankind thou hast been afflicted, and in the sufferings of thy people it was thy body that was crucified.*

A Master Fact

MATTHEW 4:17

Repent, for the kingdom of heaven is near.

The kingdom of God is a master fact. It takes control. When the kingdom becomes a reality to us, we can not live on in the old way. We must repent, begin over, overhaul the values of life and put them down at their true price, and so readjust our fundamental directions. The conduct of the individual must rise in response to higher conceptions of the meaning and possibilities of the life of humanity. Tolstoy has described his conversion in the simplest terms: "Five years ago faith came to me; I believed in the doctrine of Jesus, and my whole life underwent a sudden transformation. What I had once wished for I wished for no longer, and I began to desire what I had never desired before. What had once appeared to me right now became wrong, and the wrong of the past I beheld as right. My life and my desires were completely changed; good and evil interchanged meanings. Why so? Because I understood the words of Jesus, and life and death ceased to be evil; instead of despair, I tasted joy and happiness."

We thank thee that we have tasted the rich life of humanity. We bless thee for every hour of life, for all our share in the joys and strivings of our sisters and brothers, for the wisdom gained which will be part of us forever.

What Makes Goodness Good?

JOHN 17:20-26

*I do not pray for them alone, but for those also who believe
in me through their word, that they may all be one, even as thou,
Father, art in me and I in thee; that they also may be in us;
in order that the world may believe that thou hast sent me.*

Jesus bade us "seek first God's kingdom and righteousness," and he obeyed his own call. The main object of his
life was the ideal social order and the perfect ethic. Now if
Jesus is our ideal of human goodness, is any goodness good
unless it works in the same direction? If a person is of flaw-
less private life, but is indifferent to any social ideal, or even
hostile to all attempts at better justice and greater kinship,
is that person really good? Even a strong desire for personal
perfection, if there is no desire for a regeneration of society
in it, must be rated as sub-Christian because it is lacking in
the sense of solidarity and may be lacking in love.

*Help us make the welfare of all the supreme law of the
land, that so our commonwealth may be built strong and
secure on the love of all its citizens.*

An Ethics of Property

LUKE 18:18-25

*How hard it is for those who have money
to enter the kingdom of God!*

We need a Christian ethics of property, more perhaps than anything else. The wrongs connected to wealth are the most vulnerable point of our civilization. Unless we can make that crooked place straight, all our charities and religion are involved in hypocrisy.

We have to harmonize the two facts, that wealth is good and necessary and that wealth is a danger to its possessor and to society. On the one hand, property is indispensable to personal freedom, to all higher individuality, and to self-realization; the right to property is a corollary of the right to life; without property people are at the mercy of nature and in bondage to those who have property. On the other hand, property is used as a means of collecting tribute and private taxes, as a club with which to extort unearned gain from laborers and consumers, and as the fundamental tool of oppression.

Where do we draw the line?

Cast down the throne of Mammon who ever grinds the life of people, and set up thy throne, O Christ, for thou didst die that all might live.

Social Evil and
Social Salvation

PHILIPPIANS 3:17–4:1

*Stand fast, brothers and sisters, dearly loved and longed for,
my joy and my crown, so stand fast in the Lord, beloved!*

If evil is socialized, salvation must be socialized. The organization of the Christian Church is a recognition of the social factor in salvation. It is not enough to have God, and Christ, and the Bible. A group is needed, organized on Christian principles, and expressing the Christian spirit, which will assimilate the individual and gradually make her or him into a citizen of the kingdom of God.

Of course the question is how intensively Christian the Church can make its members. That will depend on the question how Christian the Church itself is, and there's the rub.

O God, we pray for thy Church, which is set today amid the perplexities of a changing order, and face to face with a great new task.

The Convictions of Jesus

COLOSSIANS 2:6-7

As then you have received Jesus Christ, your Lord,
in him live your lives; since you are rooted in him,
and in him continually built up.

Three convictions were axiomatic within Jesus, so that all his reasoning and his moral imperatives were based on them, just as all thought and work in physics is based on gravitation. These convictions were the sacredness of life and personality, the solidarity of the human family, and the obligation of the strong to stand up for all whose life is impaired or whose place within humanity is denied.

It can not be questioned that these convictions were a tremendous and spontaneous force in the spirit of Jesus.

The more vividly these spiritual convictions glow in the heart of any of us, the more will we feel that Jesus is still ahead, still the inspiring force. As soon as we get beyond theory to life and action, we know that we are dependent for the spiritual powers in modern life on the continued influence of Jesus Christ over the lives of others.

O God, we know that all our prayers can never bring back the past, and no tears can wash out the red marks with which we have scarred some life that stands before our memory with accusing eyes. Grant that at least a humble and pure life may grow out of our late contribution, that in the brief days still left to us we may comfort and heal where we have scorned and crushed.

Think What It Would Signify

LUKE 4:38-44

At sunset all they who had any sick with any sort
of disease brought them to Jesus; and he laid his hands
on every one of them and healed them.

Christians have never fully understood Christianity. A purer comprehension of its tremendous contents is always necessary. Think what it would signify to a local community if all sincere Christian people in it should interpret their obligation in social terms; if they should seek not only their own salvation, but the reign of God in their own town; if they should cultivate the habit of seeing a divine sacredness in every personality, should assist in creating the economic foundations for communal solidarity; and if, as Christians, they should champion the weak in their own community.

Grant us a vision of our city, fair as she might be: a city of justice, where none shall prey on others; a city of plenty, where vice and poverty shall cease to fester; a city of kinship, where all success shall be founded on service, and honor shall be given to nobleness alone; a city of peace, where order shall not rest on force, but on the love of all for the city.

The Kingdom of God

LUKE 17:20-21

The kingdom of God is now in your midst.

Jesus was the initiator of the kingdom of God. It is a real thing, now in operation. It is within us, and among us, gaining ground in our intellectual life and in our social institutions. It overlaps and interpenetrates all existing organizations, raising them to a higher level when they are good, resisting them when they are evil, quietly revolutionizing the old social order and changing it into the new. It suffers terrible reverses, but after a time it may become apparent that a master hand has turned the situation and laid the basis of victory on the wrecks of defeat. The kingdom of God is always coming; you can never lay your hand on it and say, "It is here." But such fragmentary realizations of it as we have, alone make life worth living. The memories which are still sweet and dear when the fire begins to die in the ashes, are the memories of days when we lived fully in the kingdom of Heaven, toiling for it, suffering for it, and feeling the stirring of the godlike and eternal life within us. The most humiliating and crushing realization is that we have betrayed our heavenly Homeland and sold out for thirty pieces of silver. We often mistake it. We think we see its banner in the distance, when it is only the bloody flag of the old order. But we learn. We come to know whether we are in God's country, especially if we see the great Leader near us.

Make us determined to live by truth and not by lies, to found our common life on the eternal foundations of righteousness and love, and no longer to prop the tottering house of wrong by legalized cruelty and force.

We Are Involved in Tragedy

ISAIAH 6:1-5

*Woe is me! I am lost, for I am a man of unclean lips,
and I live among a people of unclean lips; yet my eyes
have seen the King, the LORD of hosts!* (NRSV)

When we are within the presence and consciousness of
God, we see ourselves and our past actions and present
conditions in the most searching light and in eternal con-
nections. To lack the consciousness of sin is a symptom of
moral immaturity or of an effort to keep the shutters down
and the light out. The most highly developed individuals,
who have the power of interpreting life for others, and who
have the clearest realization of possible perfection and the
keenest hunger for righteousness, also commonly have the
most poignant sense of their own shortcomings.

By our very nature we are involved in tragedy . . . The
weakness or the stubbornness of our will and the tempting
situations of life combine to weave the tragic web of sin
and failure of which we all make experience before we are
through with our years.

*Give us thine inflexible sternness against sin and thine
inexhaustible compassion for the frailty and tragedy of
those who do the sin.*

The Kingdom of Evil

HEBREWS 5:11-14

*Solid food is for adults, that is, for those who
by constant practice have their faculties trained
to discriminate between good and evil.*

Human society has leaders who know what they want, but many of them have manipulated the fate of thousands for their selfish ends. The sheep-tick hides in the wool of the sheep and taps the blood where it flows warm and rich. But the tick has no power to alter the arterial system of the sheep and to bring the aorta close to the skin where it can get at it. Human ticks have been able to do this. They have gained control of legislation, courts, police, military, royalty, church, property, religion, and have altered the constitution of nations in order to make things easy for the tick class. The laws, institutions, doctrines, literature, art, and manners which these ruling classes have secreted have been social means of infection which have bred new evils for generations.

This is what the modern social gospel would call the kingdom of Evil.

Save our people from being dragged down into vaster guilt and woe by those who have no vision and know no law except their lust. Shake their souls with awe of thee that they may cease.

Solidarity of Guilt

MATTHEW 23:1-39

*Woe unto you, hypocrites! For you tithe mint and
anise and cumin, and neglect the weightier matters
of the Law—justice and mercy and good faith;
these latter you ought to have done.*

At the close of his great invective against the religious leaders of his nation, Jesus has a solidaristic vision of the spiritual unity of the generations. He warns his contemporaries
that by doing over again the acts of their forbearers, they
will bring upon them not only the blood they shed themselves, but the righteous blood shed long before. By solidarity of action and spirit we enter into solidarity of guilt. This
applies to our spiritual unity with our contemporaries. If in
the most restricted sphere of life we act on the same sinful
principles of greed and tyranny on which the great exploiters and despots act, we share their guilt. If we consent to
the working principles of the kingdom of Evil, and do not
counteract it with all our strength, but perhaps even fail to
see its ruinous evil, then we are part of it and the salvation
of Christ has not yet set us free.

*We cry to thee for justice, O Lord, for our soul is weary
with the iniquity of greed.*

The Begetting Church

MATTHEW 10:5-15

As you go, preach, saying, "The kingdom of heaven is at hand."
Heal the sick, raise the dead, cleanse the lepers,
cast out demons. Freely you have received, freely give.

If Christ is not in the Church, how does it differ from "the world"? It will still assimilate its members, but it will not make them persons bearing the family likeness of the first-born son of God.

Wherever the Church has lost the saving influence of Christ, it has lost its saltiness and is a tasteless historical survival. The saving power of the Church does not rest on its institutional character, on its continuity, its ordination, its ministry, or its doctrine. It rests on the presence of the kingdom of God within her. The Church grows old; the kingdom is ever young. The Church is a perpetuation of the past; the kingdom is the power of the coming age. Unless the Church is vitalized by the ever nascent forces of the kingdom within her, she deadens instead of begetting.

May naught mar the joy of our fellowship. May none remain lonely and hungry of heart among us. Let none go hence without the joy of new friendships. Give us the capacity for love and a richer consciousness of being loved.

The Task That Is a Gift

LUKE 21:29-36

When you see all these things coming to pass,
you will know that the kingdom of God is near.

Since God is in it, the kingdom of God is always both present and future. Like God, it is in all tenses, eternal in the midst of time. It is the energy of God realizing itself in human life. Its future lies among the mysteries of God . . . It is for us to see the kingdom of God as always coming, always pressing in on the present, always big with possibility, and always inviting immediate action. We walk by faith. Every human life is so placed that it can share with God in the creation of the kingdom, or can resist and retard its progress. The kingdom is for each of us the supreme task and the supreme gift of God. By accepting it as a task, we experience it as a gift. By laboring for it we enter into the joy and peace of the kingdom as our divine homeland and habitation.

Help us, O Lord, in the courage of faith to seize the kingdom that has now come so near, that the glad day of God may dawn at last.

The Charismatic Life of the Church

ACTS 2:1-18

They were all filled with the Holy Spirit.

The Christian Church began its history as a community of inspiration. The new thing in the story of Pentecost is not only the number of those who received the tongue of fire but the fact that the Holy Spirit had become the common property of a group. The Spirit was poured out on all flesh; the young saw visions, the old dreamed dreams; even on the slave class the Spirit was poured. The charismatic life of the primitive Church was highly important for its coherence and loyalty in the crucial days of its beginning. It was a chief feeder of its strong affections, its power of testimony, and its sacrificial spirit. Religion has been defined as "the life of God in the soul of man." In Christianity it became also the life of God in the fellowship of humankind. The mystic experience was socialized.

Grant that in the happy exchange of thought and affection we may realize anew that all our gladness comes from the simple fellowship of our human kind, and that we are rich as long as we are loved.

The Mob Spirit

ACTS 19:23-41

*Now some were shouting one thing, some another,
for the assembly was in an uproar, and the majority had
no idea why they were come together.*

The mob spirit is the social spirit gone mad. The social group then escapes from the control of its wiser and fairer habits, and is lashed into action by primitive passions. The social spirit reacts so powerfully on individuals, that when once the restraints of self-criticism and self-control are shot back, the crowd gets drunk on the mere effluvia of its own emotions. We know only too well that a city of respectable and religious people will do fiendish acts of cruelty and obscenity.

There are radical mobs and conservative mobs. Well-dressed mobs are more dangerous than ragged mobs because they are far more efficient. Entire nations may come under the mob spirit, and abdicate their judgment.

Rarely are mobs wholly spontaneous; usually there is leadership to fanaticize the masses . . . Sometimes the crowd turns against the oligarchy; usually the oligarchy manipulates the crowd.

Bring to an end, O Lord, the inhumanity of the present, in which all people are ridden by the pale fear of want while the nation of which they are citizens sits throned amid the wealth of their making.

Religious Bigotry

EPHESIANS 3:14-19

*I kneel before the Father from whom every family
in heaven or on earth takes its name.* (Goodspeed)

The persecutions of the Roman Empire against Christians were feeble and occasional as compared with the zeal of the Inquisition. It takes religion to put a steel edge on social intolerance. Just because it is so high and its command of social loyalty so great, it is pitiless when it goes wrong.

Religious bigotry has been one of the permanent evils of humankind, the cause of untold social division, bitterness, persecution, and religious wars. It is always a social sin. Estimate the harm which the exponents of religion have done simply by suppressing the prophetic minds who had received from God fresh thought on spiritual and intellectual problems, and by cowing those who might have followed the prophets.

Thou hast called our people to freedom, but we are withholding from men and women their share of the common heritage without which freedom becomes a hollow name.

The Sin Borne by Jesus

MARK 14:1-2, 53-56

*The high priests and the Scribes were casting about
for a way to arrest him by stealth and put him to death.*
(Goodspeed)

Jesus was killed by ecclesiastical religion. He might have appeared in almost any highly developed nation and suffered the same fate. Certainly after religion bore his name, there were a thousand situations in which he would have been put to death by those who offered salvation in his name. Innumerable individuals contribute their little quota to make up this collective evil, and when once the common mind is charged with it, it gets innumerable outlets. This sin, then, was borne by Jesus, not by imputation, nor by sympathy, but by direct experience.

Thou hast been wounded by our transgressions and bruised by our iniquities, and all our sins are laid at last on thee. Amid the groaning of creation we behold thy Spirit in travail till the children of God shall be born in freedom and holiness.

Bound Together with Love

JOHN 13:1; 15:12-17

*Jesus, knowing that his hour was come when he should
leave this world to go to his Father, having loved his own
who were in the world, showed forth his love to the end.*

The death of Christ was the supreme revelation of love.

Love is the social instinct of humanity. In all its many
forms it binds person to person. Every real improvement
of society gives love a freer chance. Every genuine progress
must be preceded by a new capitalization of love.

Jesus put love to the front of his teaching. He was ready
to accept love for God and humanity as a valid equivalent
for the customary religious and ethical duties. His own
character and action are redolent of virile and energetic
love.

His death underscored all he said on love. It put the red
seal of sincerity on his words. "No one has greater love
than this, to lay down one's life for one's friends." Unless
one gives it for one's enemies too.

*Grant to the rulers of nations faith in the possibility of
peace through justice, and grant to the common people
a new and stern enthusiasm for the cause of peace. Bless
our soldiers and sailors for their swift obedience and their
willingness to answer the call of duty, but inspire them
nonetheless with a hatred of war, and may they never for
love of private glory or advancement provoke its coming.*

God in the Midst of Us

JOHN 1:1-5, 14

*In the beginning was the Word, and the Word was
face to face with God, and the Word was God. All things
came into being through him, and apart from him nothing that
exists came into being. In him was life, and the life was the
light of all people. And the light is shining in the darkness,
and the darkness has not overwhelmed it. And the Word
became flesh and tented with us. And we gazed on his glory—
glory as of the Father's only Son—full of grace and truth.*

God is not only the spiritual representative of humanity;
God is identified with humanity. In God we live and move
and have our being. In us God lives and moves, though
God's being transcends ours. God is the life and the light
in every soul and the mystic bond that unites us all. God
is the spiritual power behind and beneath all our aspirations and achievements. God works through humanity to
realize divine purposes, and our sins block and destroy the
Reign of God in which God seeks to be revealed and realized. Therefore our sins against the least of our brothers
and sisters in the last resort concern God. Therefore when
we retard the progress of humankind, we retard the revelation of the glory of God. Our universe is not a despotic
monarchy, with God above the starry canopy and ourselves
down here; it is a spiritual commonwealth with God in the
midst of us.

We pray thee to revive in us the hardy spirit of our fore-bears that we may establish and complete their work, building on the basis of their democracy the firm edifice of a cooperative commonwealth, in which both government and industry shall be of the people, by the people, and for the people.

Turning

PSALM 139:23-24

*See if there be any wicked way in me, and lead me
in the ancient way.* (NRSV)

Sin is the greatest preacher of repentance. Give it time, and
it will cool our lust in shame. When God wants to halt the
prideful who are going wrong, God lets them go to the full
length and find out the latter end for themselves. That is
what God has done with our nation in its headlong ride on
the road of covetousness. Mammonism stands convicted by
its own works. It was time for us to turn.

We are turning.

Were you ever converted to God? Do you remember the
change in your attitude to all the world? Is not this new life
which is running through our people the same great change
on a national scale? This is religious energy, rising from the
depth of that infinite spiritual life in which we all live and
move and have our being. This is God.

*Purge our cities and states and nation of the deep causes
of corruption which have so often made sin profitable and
uprightness hard. Bring to an end the stale days of political party cunning.*

New Hope of a Better Day

ROMANS 15:1-7, 13

*Now the God of patience and of comfort grant you to be in
full sympathy with one another, in accordance with the example
of Jesus Christ; so that with one heart and with one voice you
may glorify the God and Father of our Lord Jesus Christ.*

The other day I was walking along the seashore. A broad
stretch of sand and slimy stones was between me and the
water. Dead things lay about, stranded, limp, and gray. It
was ebb tide.

When I returned after a few hours, a magic change had
taken place. Over the stagnant flats the waves were rolling
briskly and eagerly, as if they were young. The gulls were
dipping and screaming. Gray ripples far out showed where
fish were schooling. All the world smelled and felt differ-
ently. The tide was coming in.

The same sense of great change comes over anyone who
watches the life of this nation with an eye for the stirring of
God in the souls of men and women. There is a new shame
and anger for oppression and meanness; a new love and
pity for the young and frail whose slender shoulders bear
our common weight; a new faith in human kinship; a new
hope of a better day that is even now in sight.

*Breathe a new spirit into all our nation. Give our leaders
a new vision of the possible future of our country and set
their hearts on fire with large resolves. Raise up a new
generation of public leaders who will have the faith and
daring of the kingdom of God in their hearts and who will
enlist for life in a holy warfare for the freedom and rights
of the people.*

Christianizing the Social Order

MATTHEW 5:1-12

*When Jesus saw the crowds, he went up the mountain,
and when he had seated himself, his disciples came to him,
and opening his lips he began to teach them.*

By Christianizing the social order I do not mean putting the name of Christ into the Constitution of the United States . . . In the present stage of our life that would only be one more act of national hypocrisy.

Neither do we want to set up a theocracy ruled by the Church and making Christian belief and worship a compulsory duty of citizenship. All the experience of history protests against coercion in religion.

Christianizing the social order means bringing it into harmony with the ethical convictions which we identify with Christ. Christianizing means humanizing in the highest sense.

O God, who art the author and giver of law, from whom alone all just designs and righteous judgments proceed, give unto all those who frame, interpret, or administer human law the counsel of thy Holy Spirit that they may know themselves thy ministers.

Beauty

PSALM 27:4

To behold the beauty of the LORD. (NRSV)

God's country is the home of beauty. God is not only the all-vocal and all-powerful but the all-beautiful. The connection between religion and beauty, between morality and art, is of the closest. The sense of beauty is the morning portal of the temple of God by which the young best love to enter for worship. Ruskin has taught us that art has its roots in the moral life, and that permanent ugliness is a product of sin and a producer of brutality.

The redeemed portions of our social order all cultivate beauty. There are few homes so poor that you will not find some attempt at beauty for its own sake. In our churches religion long ago entered into partnership with architecture, music, and color. Schools are decorating their walls with pictures. Our cities and states are developing beauty in their parks and public buildings.

How do capitalistic industry and commerce deal with the aesthetic life? Human labor beautifies nature. But I have revisited countrysides that I knew in wooded glory in my boyhood, and have found the trees slashed out and the mountain looking like a house rifled by burglars. Nature, our common mother, sits like a captive queen among barbarians who are tearing the jewels from her hair. Beauty that ages have fashioned and that no human skill can replace is effaced to enrich a few persons whose enrichment is of little use to anybody.

O thou who art the all-pervading glory of the world, we bless thee for the power of beauty to gladden our hearts. We praise thee that even the least of us may feel a thrill of thy creative joy when we give form and substance to our thoughts and, beholding our handiwork, find it good and fair.

No One Stands Alone

MATTHEW 6:9-13

This is the way you are to pray. (Goodspeed)

The Lord's Prayer is recognized as the purest expression of the mind of Jesus. It crystallizes his thoughts. It gives proof of the transparent clearness and peace of his soul. When he bade us say, "Our Father," Jesus spoke from that consciousness of human solidarity which was a matter of course in all his thinking. He compels us to clasp hands in spirit with all our sisters and brothers and thus to approach God together. This rules out all selfish isolation in religion. Before God no one stands alone. Before the All-Seeing we each are surrounded by the spiritual throng of all to whom we stand related near and far, all whom we love or hate, whom we serve or oppress, whom we wrong or save. We are one with our fellows in all our needs. We are one in our sin and salvation. To realize this oneness is the first step toward praying the Lord's Prayer aright.

O thou great Champion of the outcast and the weak,
we remember before thee the people of other nations
who are coming to our land seeking bread, a home, and
a future. May we look with thy compassion upon them.
For we, too, are the children of immigrants who came
with anxious hearts and halting feet on the path of hope.

The Word Must Become Flesh

JAMES 1:19-25

*Strip yourselves of everything that soils you,
and every evil growth, and in a humble spirit let the
message that has the power to save your souls be planted in
your hearts. Obey the message; do not merely listen to it,
and deceive yourselves.* (Goodspeed)

Christianity must offer every person a full salvation. The individualistic gospel never did this. Its evangelism never recognized more than a fractional part of the saving forces at work in God's world. Salvation was often whittled down to a mere doctrinal proposition; assent to that, and you are saved. Social Christianity holds to all the real values in the old methods but rounds them out to meet all the needs of human life.

Salvation is always a social process. It comes by human contact. The word must become flesh if it is to save. Some man or woman, or some group of people, in whom the saving love of Jesus Christ has found a new incarnation, lays hold of an enfeebled, blinded human atom and infuses new hope and courage and insight, new warmth of love and strength of will, and there is a new breathing of the soul and an opening of the inner eye. Salvation has begun.

O Jesus, may no reckless word or wanton look from me kindle the slow fires of wayward passion that will char and consume the divine beauties of any soul.

An Absolute Claim of Obedience

LUKE 6:46-49

*Why are you calling me Lord, Lord,
and not doing what I tell you?*

Jesus never transferred the kingdom hope from earth to heaven. Neither did he ever spiritualize the vitality out of the kingdom idea, as the Church has so constantly done. It was never a disembodied ghost to him, but a warm and lovable human reality. The purpose of all that Jesus said and did and hoped to do was always the social redemption of the entire life of the human race on earth. If we regard him in any sense as our leader and master, we cannot treat as secondary what to him was the essence of his mission. If we regard him as the Son of God, the revelation of the very mind and will and nature of the Eternal, the obligation to complete what he began comes upon us with an absolute claim to obedience.

To our whole nation do thou grant wisdom to create a world in which none shall be forced to idle in want, and none shall be able to idle in luxury, but in which all shall know the health of wholesome work and the sweetness of well-earned rest.

Jesus and His Enemies

1 CORINTHIANS 1:17-25

*The message of the Cross is indeed for those on their
way to destruction, foolishness; but for us who are on
our way to salvation, it is the power of God.*

The Jesus with whom his enemies dealt, and from whom
they backed away, was never very passive. He was high-
power energy from first to last. His death itself was action.
It was the most terrific blow that organized evil ever got. He
always moved with a purpose and his purpose always was
the kingdom of God. At the beginning he really hoped to
win his nation. When he saw isolation and death impend-
ing, he accepted the law of vicarious suffering as part of
the method of redemption, and took Death by the hand
as God's minister to bring in the kingdom. His death was
his greatest act of social service. His cross was the climax
of the world evil and the turning point of history toward
a definite and permanent emancipation and redemption
of the human race. All the great permanent forces of evil
in humanity were strangely combined in the drama of his
death: bigotry, despotism, political corruption, militarism,
and the mob spirit. They converged on him and did him to
death. But he is alive, and now it is their turn.

*May those who entrap the feet of the weak and make
their living by the degradation of people thrust away their
shameful gains and stand clear. But if their conscience is
silenced by profit, do thou grant thy people the indomita-
ble strength of faith to make an end of it.*

Life Is Miraculous

PSALM 103

*Bless the L*ORD*, O my soul, and all that is within me,*
bless his holy name, who forgives, who heals, who redeems,
who crowns you with steadfast love and mercy,
who satisfies you with good as long as you live. (NRSV)

It is no slight achievement of faith to think of God immanent in the whole vast universe, but those who accomplish
that act of faith feel God very near and mysteriously present, pulsating in their own souls in every yearning for truth
and love and right. Life once more becomes miraculous; for
every event in which we realize God and our soul is a mir-
acle. All history becomes the unfolding of the purpose of
the immanent God who is working in the race toward the
commonwealth of spiritual liberty and righteousness. History is the sacred workshop of God. Thousands of young
minds who thought a few years ago that they had turned
their backs on religion forever are full of awe and a sense of
mystery as they watch the actualities of life in this process
of upbuilding. By cooperating with God in the work of God
they are realizing God. Religion is insuppressible.

May we realize that all the living things live, not for us
alone, but for themselves and for thee, and that they love
the sweetness of life, even as we, and serve thee in their
place better than we in ours.

God's Country

ISAIAH 61:1-4

*The Spirit of the LORD God is upon me . . . to give
unto them beauty for ashes, the oil of joy for mourning,
the garment of praise for the spirit of heaviness; that
they might be called trees of righteousness, the planting
of the LORD, that he might be glorified. (KJV)*

Life is a sacred spark of God in us . . . Wherever life is held precious, and restored and redeemed when broken or soiled, there is God's country, and there the law of Christ prevails. But in our economic system life is held cheap and wasted needlessly, and the play and beauty of life are turned into weariness. Death rules because love and solidarity do not rule. One is set against another in two classes, of which one can flourish in luxury, while the other toils in want. The exhaustive toil and the want of the one class may even be the means to speed and pile up the wealth of the other. The Profit of the Few has turned against the Life of the Many. God's reign will not come until the profit of all shall support the life of all.

Save our nation from the corruption that breeds corruption. We remember with sorrow and compassion the idle rich, who have vigor of body and mind and yet produce no useful thing. Forgive them for loading the burden of their support on the bent shoulders of the working world. Forgive them for wasting in refined excess what would feed the pale children of the poor. . . . We beseech thee to awaken them by the new voice of thy Spirit that they may look up into the stern eyes of thy Christ and may be smitten with the blessed pangs of repentance.

Artists as Revolutionists

GENESIS 1:1–2:4

In the beginning when God created the heavens and the earth, the earth was a formless void and darkness covered the face of the deep, while a wind from God swept over the face of the waters. (NRSV)

Our economic system is not a sincere friend of beauty either in nature or art. If profit beckons, the beauties of nature are blotted out without remorse. If profit beckons, art is used, but only to be soiled somewhat. For the real development of beauty we need communities that have wealth of their own, a great public with leisure and culture enough to enjoy art, and a working class with leisure and vitality enough to develop the artistic talent in gifted individuals. Why have so many artists been revolutionists at heart?

Teach all those in the arts that they, too, are but servants of humanity, and that the promise of their gifts can fulfill itself only in the service of love. Kindle in their hearts a passionate pity for the joyless lives of the people, and make them rejoice if they are found worthy to hold the cup of beauty to lips that are athirst. Make them the reverent interpreters of God to humankind, who see thy face and hear thy voice in all things, that so they may unveil for us the beauties of nature which we have passed unseeing, and the sadness and sweetness of humanity to which our selfishness has made us blind.

A Synonym of Love

ROMANS 12:9-21

Let love be without insincerity. Abhor what is evil;
wed yourselves to what is good. Be tenderly affectionate
one to another, in honor preferring one another.

One of the glories of Christianity is the place it gives to love. It sums up all religious duty in love to God, and all ethical duty in love to others. It has set before humanity as the fullest revelation of God and the highest expression of personhood the life of Jesus Christ, whose name is a synonym of love. It has made love the dominant characteristic in the nature of God, and therewith has written love across the whole universe.

Love is the force that draws one to another, the great social instinct of human beings. The social mission of Christianity is to make this natural instinct strong, durable, pure, holy, and victorious over all selfish and hateful passions. The spirit of Christ allies itself with all other social forces that make for love. It is at enmity with anything that checks love or propagates hate.

Suffer us not to cherish dark thoughts of resentment or revenge. So fill us with thy abounding love and peace that no ill-will may be left in our hearts.

Capitalism or Christ?

LUKE 16:1-13

No one can be a household servant to two masters;
for either the person will hate the one and love the other,
or will cling to the one and despise the other.
You cannot be the slave both of God and of gold.

Whoever declares the law of Christ is impracticable in actual life, or has to be superseded in business by the laws of capitalism, to that extent dethrones Christ and enthrones Mammon. When we try to keep both enthroned at the same time in different sections of our lives, we do what Christ says cannot be done, and accept a double life as the normal morality for our nation and for many individuals in it . . . The most comprehensive and intensive act of love in which we could share would be a collective action of the community to change the present organization of the economic life into a new order that would rest on the Christian principles of equal rights, democratic distribution of economic power, the supremacy of the common good, the law of mutual dependence and service, and the uninterrupted flow of good will throughout the human family.

Behold the servants of Mammon, who have brought upon thy church the contempt of people and have cloaked their extortion with the gospel of thy Christ.

Mummery Churches

MARK 2:18-22

No one ever pours new wine into old wine-skins,
else the wine would burst the skins, and both wine and skins
would be lost. New wine is poured into fresh wine-skins.

The process of Christianizing the Church is not yet complete. To become fully Christian the churches must turn their back on dead issues and face their present tasks. There is probably not a single denomination which is not thrusting on its people questions for which no one would care and of which only antiquarians would know if the churches did not keep these questions alive. Our children sometimes pull the clothes of their grandparents out of old chests in the attic and masquerade in long-tailed coats or crinolines. We religious folks who air the issues of the sixteenth century go through the same mummery in solemn earnest, while the enemy is at the gate. One of the most practical means for Christianizing the social order is to multiply the number of minds who have turned in conscious repentance from the old maxims, the old admirations, and the old desires, and have accepted for good and all the Christian law with all that it implies for modern conditions.

O Jesus, if in our loyalty to the Church of the past we
have distrusted thy living voice and have suffered thee to
pass from our door unheard, we pray thee forgive us. If
ever we have been more concerned for the strong and the
rich than for the shepherdless throngs of the people for
whom thy soul grieved, we pray thee to forgive us.

The Salvation of the Church

REVELATION 3:14-22

Let everyone who can hear listen to what
the Spirit says to the churches. (Goodspeed)

To become fully Christian the Church must come out of its spiritual isolation. In theory and practice the Church has long constituted a world by itself. It has been governed by ecclesiastical motives and interests which are often remote from the real interests of humanity, and has almost uniformly set church questions ahead of social questions . . . It has offered peace and spiritual tranquility to men and women who needed thunderclaps and lightning. Like all the rest of us, the Church will get salvation by finding the purpose of its existence outside itself, in the kingdom of God, the perfect life of humanity.

May all the great churches of our land shake off those
who seek the shelter of religion for that which damns,
and stand with level front against their common foe. May
all who still soothe their souls with half-truths, saying,
"Peace, peace," where there can be no peace, learn to see
through thy stern eyes and come to the help of Jehovah
against the mighty.

The Church Must Be Liberated

JAMES 4:1-10

You renegades! Do you not know that the friendship of the world means enmity with God? (Goodspeed)

To become fully Christian the Church must still further emancipate itself from the dominating forces of the present era. In an age of political despotism our forebears cut the Church loose from state control and state support, and therewith released the moral forces of progress. In an age of financial autocracy, we must be far more watchful than we have been lest we bargain away the spiritual freedom of the Church for opulent support.

It takes great faith to believe that the Church will gain life by losing life. But as surely as the law of the Cross is the supreme law of the Church, she will sicken and die of old age if she shrinks from her burden and quenches the Spirit which is plainly speaking to her soul; and she will renew her youth and mount to a Christlike spirituality never reached before, if she will freely and without compulsion take up the cause of the people and follow the Lord on the *Via Dolorosa*.

Fill thy Church with the prophets' scorn of tyranny, and with a Christlike tenderness for the heavy-laden and down-trodden.

As Jesus Desired

EPHESIANS 1:3-10

God has given us perfect insight into his secret purpose and understanding of it, in following out the design he planned to carry out in Christ, and in arranging, when the time should have fully come, that everything in heaven and on earth should be unified in Christ. (Goodspeed)

If production could be organized as a basis of cooperative fraternity; if distribution could at least approximately be determined by justice; if everyone could be conscious that their labor contributed to the welfare of all and that their personal well-being was dependent on the prosperity of the commonwealth; if predatory business and parasitic wealth ceased and everyone lived only by their labor; if the luxury of unearned wealth no longer made us feverish with covetousness and a simpler life became the fashion; if our time and strength were not used up either in getting a bare living or in amassing unusable wealth and we had more leisure for the higher pursuits of the mind and the soul—then there might be a chance to live such a life of gentleness and kindness and tranquility of heart as Jesus desired for all people.

O God, we thank thee for the abundance of our blessings, but we pray that our plenty may not involve want for others. Do thou satisfy the desire of every child of thine.

Extensions of the Kingdom

REVELATION 1:4-6

*To Him who loves us and has loosed us from our sins
in his own blood; and has made us to be a kingdom
of priests unto his God and Father; to him be the glory
and dominion forever and ever.*

The efforts for the extension of the kingdom of God are insufficient if they address themselves to the individual alone. A world of regenerated individuals is not necessarily a regenerated world. The laws of nations, the customs of society, the institutions of corporate life, though indirectly affected by every personal change, may perpetuate wrong and warp the individuals, and a conscious effort must be made to reconstruct them, until they cease to be based on selfishness and force and begin to be based on love and justice. Every step toward such reconstruction, as well as every individual conversion, is an extension of the reign of God, for God reigns where God's will is done.

O thou great source of truth and knowledge, we remember before thee all whose calling it is to gather and winnow the facts for informing the people. Inspire them with a determined love for honest work and a staunch hatred for the making of lies, lest the judgments of our nation be perverted and we be taught to call light darkness and darkness light.

The Universal Power of Love

1 CORINTHIANS 13:7, 8, 13

*Love knows how to be silent, it is trustful, hopeful,
patient, enduring. Love never fails.*

In all its forms love creates an enjoyment of contact and a desire for more of it, a sense of the worth and human beauty of those we love, pride in their advancement, joy in their happiness, pain in their suffering, a consciousness of unity, an identity of interests, an instinctive realization of solidarity.

This is the wide sense in which we must use the word "love" if we are to realize the incomparable power and value of love in human life. Our understanding of life depends on our comprehension of the universal power of love. Our capacity to build society depends on our power of calling out love. Our faith in God and Christ is measured by our faith in the value and workableness of love.

Hallow all our joys, and if there is anything wanton or unholy in them, open our eyes that we may see. If we have ever gained our bread by injustice, or eaten it in heartlessness, cleanse our life and give us a spirit of humility and love, that we may be worthy to sit at the common table of humanity in the great house of our Father.

The Charge of Hypocrisy

AMOS 5:6-15

*Seek good and not evil, that you may live. Hate evil
and love good, and establish justice.* (NRSV)

When injustice becomes widespread and permanent, it
undoes the Christian character of the social order, because it
makes human solidarity impossible between the oppressors
and the oppressed, and because it deprives both of them of
their full Christian personhood. Those who profit by injustice become parasitic. On the other hand, the exploited are
deprived of an equal opportunity to develop their gifts.
Something of the divine life in them is suppressed. If the
church looks on injustice without holy anger it allows the
institution of redemptive love to give shelter to lovelessness,
and is itself involved in the charge of hypocrisy.

*As we have mastered nature that we might gain wealth,
help us now to master the social relations of humankind
that we may gain justice and a world of brothers and sisters. For what shall it profit our nation if it gain numbers
and riches, and lose the sense of the living God and the joy
of human kinship?*

Gathered in Christ's Name

MATTHEW 18:15-20

*Wherever there are two or three gathered together
in my name, there am I among them.*

It stands to reason that religion demands social expression, and will come to its full strength and richness only when it is shared with others. And so in fact we find it. There is a sweetness in private prayer, but there is an additional thrill when we join in a heartfelt hymn and are swept on the wave crest of a common emotion. Most of us have come to the great religious decision in life only under the influence of social emotion. With most of us the flame of religious longing and determination would flicker lower and lower in the course of the years if it were not fanned afresh by contact with the experiences and the religious willpower of others. When Jesus said that where two or three are gathered in his name, he is in the midst of them, he expressed the profound truth that his presence is fully realized only in a Christian society; it may be a very small group, but it needs at least one other human heart next to ours to be fully sensible of the Christ.

Into thy keeping we commit our friends, and pray that we may never lose their love by losing thee.

Something Heavenly in Children

MATTHEW 18:1-6

In solemn truth I tell you that unless you turn and become like little children, you will not enter the kingdom of heaven.

The child is humanity reduced to its simplest terms. Affectionate joy in children is perhaps the purest expression of social feeling. Jesus was indignant when the disciples thought children were not of sufficient importance to occupy his attention. Compared with the selfish ambition of grown-ups he felt something heavenly in children, a breath of the kingdom of God. They are nearer the kingdom than those whom the world has smudged. To inflict any spiritual injury on one of these little ones seemed to Jesus an inexpressible guilt.

Make clear to those of older years the inalienable right of childhood to play, and make clear to us all that the great school of life is not encompassed by walls and that its teachers are all who influence their younger brothers and sisters by companionship and example, whether for good or evil, and that in that school all we are teachers and as we teach are judged. For all false teaching, for all hindering of thy children, pardon us, O Lord, and suffer the little children to come unto thee, for Jesus' sake.

Intent on a Better Future

ISAIAH 11:1-9

*The earth will be full of the knowledge of the LORD
as the waters cover the sea.* (NRSV)

Capitalism is penny wise and pound foolish. Capitalism can cut down the timber which unaided nature has grown through centuries, but it cannot afford the long wait that is needed to grow new forests. It leaves the exploited timber lands and turns elsewhere for new profits. The conservation movement is a national confession that capitalism, in dealing with the natural resources of the country, is a national peril. In using up the resources of nature faster than we can replace them, we graft on our own children, for they will have to live in a land of wasted forests, gutted mines, and dried water courses. The avarice induced by our economic system sacrifices the future to immediate enrichment. From the point of view of a religious evolutionist that is one of the greatest of all sins. God and nature are always supremely intent on a better future.

We remember with shame that in the past we have exercised the high dominion of human beings with ruthless cruelty, so that the voice of the Earth, which should have gone up to thee in song, has been groaning in travail.

It Shall Be

REVELATION 21:1-7; 22:1-5

Behold, God's tent is with mortals, and he will tent with them, and they will be his peoples. And God himself with be with them. "Behold, I am making all things new. It has now come to pass. I am the Alpha and the Omega, the Beginning and the End."

Some day it shall be! All the far-off visons of the seers shall take form and substance. All that the prophet's fire-touched lip has spoken shall be true; no clash of sword; no tramp of armed people, but the glad click of scythes in the harvest field and the happy song of maidens going to their common task. No longer shall the groaning of creation rise to touch the heart of God, but peace shall be on earth, and glory shall rise to the Giver of good like the rising of the tinted morning mists.

Where once the city of Satan stood shall stand the city of God. No pall of smoke shall hang above with feeble lights to pierce it from beneath; for the glory of the Lord shall rest upon it and the Lamb shall be the light thereof. There shall be no temple there, no sacred spot or hallowed time, for all time shall be God's and all life shall be a sacrifice. Then knowledge and wisdom shall not be the heritage of few, but all shall know, and the knowledge of the Lord and the Lord's works shall cover the earth like the rolling waters of the sea. And when the people meet on the streets of that city, they shall clasp hands and say, "My brother, my sister, God is good," and the only tear that flows there is the tear of joy and adoration.

It shall be, for God reigns. It shall be, for humanity feels it afar off, and the soul of humanity is prophetic. "Watchman, what of the night?" Is thy soul awake and thine eye clear to discern the coming of the Lord? Is thy soul purified to meet his gaze? Is thy heart loving and thy brow meek? Is thy heart firm in faith and tranquil in hope?

It shall be. The kingdom of God is coming. Shall it come with or without thy help, O my brother, O my sister?

O thou who art the light of my soul, I thank thee for the incomparable joy of listening to thy voice within, and I know that no word of thine shall return void, however brokenly uttered. If aught in this book was said through lack of knowledge, or through weakness of faith in thee or of love for others, I pray thee to overrule my sin and turn aside its force before it harm thy cause. Pardon the frailty of thy servant, and look upon him only as he sinks his life in Jesus, his Master and Savior. Amen.

Quotation Sources

By Walter Rauschenbusch

CSC: *Christianity and the Social Crisis* (NY: Association Press, 1912)

CSO: *Christianizing the Social Order* (NY: Macmillan Co., 1912)

DWBC: *Dare We Be Christians?* (Boston, MA: Pilgrim Press, 1914)

PSA: *Prayers of the Social Awakening* (Boston, MA: Pilgrim Press, 1910)

ROK: *The Righteousness of the Kingdom*, Max L. Stackhouse, editor (Nashville, TN: Abingdon Press, 1968)

SL: "The Culture of the Spiritual Life," *The Rochester Baptist Monthly*, 1897

SPJ: *The Social Principles of Jesus* (NY: Association Press, 1919)

SW: *WR: Selected Writings*, Winthrop S. Hudson, editor (NY: Paulist Press, 1984)

TSG: *A Theology for the Social Gospel* (NY: Macmillan, 1917)

UM: *Unto Me* (Norwood, MA: The Pilgrim Press, 1912)

WHY: "Why I Am a Baptist," *The Baptist Leader* (January 1958) 7–17; originally published in *The Rochester Baptist Monthly* (November 1905, January 1906, February 1906, March 1906)

Secondary Source

WR: Dores Robinson Sharpe, *Walter Rauschenbusch* (NY: Macmillan Co., 1942)

Quotation References

The Inward Journey

We Live on Grace	TSG 272, 273; PSA 32, 33
The Source of Our Life	SW 105; PSA 28, 29
Strike Roots Deep in the Past	SW 105; SW 220
So Salvation Came to Me	SW 45; PSA 85
A Second Great Struggle	SW 45; PSA 84
From Sin to Salvation	TSG 97, 98; PSA 110
One Who Is Old in Quest of Truth	CSO 10, 11; SW 238
The Joy of Play	CSO 248, 249; PSA 58
Fatal Attraction	CSO 292, 459; PSA 101
Too Much!	CSO 472; PSA 39
God Is the Great Joy	CSO 473; PSA 115
The Joy of Prayer	WR 272, 273; SW 239
A Bible within the Bible	DWBC 7, 8; SW 238
The Little Chapter of Love	DWBC 9, 10; PSA 34
The Revelation of God	SW 118, 119; SW 238
The Higher Life	SL; PSA 47
Tending the Spiritual Life	SL; SW 237
My Old Christianity	WR 221, 222; PSA 109
The New Life of Faith	WHY 9; PSA 119
A Faith to Cover the Whole	WR 221; PSA 98
Fellowship of Saints	SL; PSA 35
So Diverse Yet the Same	WHY 8; SW 237
Second-hand Religion	WHY 9; PSA 82
Being and Doing	SPJ 152; PSA 75
In Times of Doubt	WHY 9; PSA 103, 104
Go into That Inner Solitude	WHY 10; SW 237
Above All Else	SW 67; PSA 104
Instructions in Case of My Death, March 1918	WR 448, 449; PSA 91, 92, 93

The Outward Journey

A Christlike Life . . .	ROK 151
The Inward and the Outward	ROK 85, 86; PSA 61
The Kingdom Touches Everything	WR 222; PSA 57
Least Wanting to Hear	ROK 168, 172; WR 203; PSA 29, 30
Sin of Omission	SW 100; PSA 27
The Privilege of Service	SW 100; SW 237
All Are Called	SW 101; PSA 29
The Question to Ask Yourself	SW104; PSA 33, 34
I Could Not Keep Silent	SW 45, CSO 117, 118; PSA 73
Show Me What to Do	SW 106; PSA 91
Love at the Center	DWBC 55, 56; PSA 30

The Common Journey